Marketing Health Care to Women

Meeting New Demands for Products and Services

Patricia Braus

American Demographics Books
Ithaca, New York

A Division of American Demographics, Inc.
127 West State Street, Ithaca, NY 14850
Telephone: 607-273-6343

Executive Editor: Diane Crispell
Managing Editor: Nancy Ten Kate
Project Coordinator: Kevin Heubusch
Project Editor: Berna Miller
Publisher: Wade Leftwich
Associate Publisher: James Madden
Fulfillment Manager: Doreen Zamoiski

Library of Congress Catalog Number:

Cataloging In Publication Data
Braus, Patricia 1957–
Marketing Health Care to Women

ISBN 0-936889-40-3

Book design and composition: Peter C. Krakow

Acknowledgements

Thanks above all to the many health and marketing experts and to the many women who kindly shared their knowledge, their data and their opinions with me. Without their generosity there would have been no book.

Sally Rynne first alerted me to the dynamic field of women's health marketing, and her knowledgeable support during this project was an immense help. Health marketers Richard Ireland, Ruthie H. Dearing and Mary Anne Graf were also helpful, as was public relations expert Kathleen L. Lewton. Though scores of experts contributed generously to the final product, certain sources were particularly helpful to my understanding of the subject. I owe special gratitude to Maxine F. Brinkman, Terry Mullady Guymon, Carol Landau Ph.D., Wendy Lund, Dr. June LaValeur, Lisa Borders Marbury, Cindy Pearson, Kris Powell, Mickey C. Smith Ph.D., Carol S. Weisman Ph.D., Deanne Williams and Margaret Wylde Ph.D.

Kimberly Weiss at The National Association of Women's Health Professionals in Chicago, enabled me to contact many of its members, whose comments help shape the book. The organizations Find/SVP of New York and About Women, Inc., of Boston, generously shared their information-rich marketing reports. Simmons Market Research, the A.C.Nielsen Co., Kline and Co., the Kaiser Family Foundation and EDK Associates also made their incisive research reports available to me.

Thanks to Brad Edmondson, editor of this book, for his unfailing good cheer and encouragement, his sound knowledge of demographics and his editorial skill. I also am grateful to Berna Miller, Kevin Heubusch, and Nancy Ten Kate for their professional editorial assistance.

A final thanks to my friends and family. Friends enthusiastically shared their experiences about everything from visits to the pediatrician to the herbalist, as well as their adventures as callers to toll-free health lines. My parents, Jane and Jay Braus, brother Paul and sister Nancy were attentive supporters. Peter Braus, another brother, generously shared his professional marketing experience. Edwin Lopez, my husband, offered many incisive comments about early versions of the book. He and our sons, Daniel and Jay, generously shared their love and encouragement from start to finish.

Table of Contents

Index of charts and tables

Chapter 8:

Chapter 9:

Preface

This book examines an important but largely ignored subject: how health care is sold to women from their teenage years to the final years of life. Most doctors, hospital administrators, pharmacists, and other health professionals know from experience that women usually control the household decision-making when it comes to health care. Yet relatively few marketers specialize in women's health care, and many health-care firms make no special efforts to reach this crucial group.

What women want from health-care providers is relatively simple, but satisfying them can be quite complex. Women want high-quality care from sensitive professionals who have the time to answer their questions at any hour of the day or night. Meanwhile, health-care providers are under increasing pressure to cut costs and boost revenues. These goals often clash. Even the most successful health marketers must balance the increasing expectations of their patients with the increasing expectations of their accountants.

The best way for health-care firms to thrive in this demanding environment is to gain a detailed knowledge of the unique wants and needs of women seeking health care. This book looks at those wants and needs at each stage of a woman's life and gives a critical examination of the products and services aimed at each stage. Special attention is given to the directors of women's health-care centers, whose innovative approach to health care can serve as a model to others. Another important group is the marketers of preventive health care, whose methods will be increasingly important as the population ages. And the future may be somewhere in the burgeoning field of alternative health therapies, which hold a strong appeal for women in their 30s, 40s, and 50s.

Women's health care is such a broad topic that including every related health product or service would be impossible in a book of this size. Women are tremendous users of mental-health products and services, for example, and they are far more likely than men to suffer from depression. The marketing of anti-depressive drugs such as Prozac has become a major public issue, with best-selling books examining the drug and its promotion. It would be unwise and unfair to include a cursory review of this huge subject in these pages. The marketing of mental health is a good topic for a book, not a single book chapter.

Other topics that are not addressed in depth include important diseases such as diabetes, which is responsible for a major industry marketing insulin-testing related products; and HIV, which is an increasing threat to women and an engine for drug development at many of the major drug companies. This book also bypasses a wealth of diseases and syndromes identified over the past few decades whose treatment has remained elusive. Women with many of these conditions, such as Premenstrual Syndrome and Chronic Fatigue Syndrome, are major consumers of conventional and alternative medical care and products. But the diversity in the way they are treated and the type of treatment used precluded focusing on them in this volume.

Women must cope with a long list of serious health conditions, not all of which can be examined here. But many of the lessons from this field can be useful to anyone who wants to sell a health product or service to women. The successful marketing of cosmetic plastic surgery, a service women do not need for medical reasons, offers lessons for physicians and hospitals that specialize in dramatically different services. Likewise, the successful but increasingly controversial marketing of hormone replacement therapy offers a guide to what women want in medical care. It also reveals what level of risk some women are unwilling to accept.

The shifting size and changing demographic profile of American women offer important clues about the products and services they will want in the future. Once you understand the basic facts about consumer demand for a product—such as the age at which users are most expected to use it—you can use the population projections in this book to get a sense of what your future customers will be like, and how many of them you can expect to serve.

The ever-changing medical field guarantees that whatever is written about medical practices, procedures, and problems will soon become outdated. When valuable new drugs and technologies are available, the expectations and needs of patients will always change. But some things will not change. Women will still approach health care in a particular way. They will remain the family decision-makers in health matters for the foreseeable future. They will continue to have an insatiable hunger for information about health. And they will be more demanding of high-quality products and services.

The rules of medicine may change rapidly, but the patients themselves change slowly. Finding better ways to cultivate women as prospective patients and customers is a constant challenge, and this book explains how it can be done.

Chapter I

Focus on Women

- A hospital in San Antonio, Texas, offers women discounts at restaurants and department stores.

- A California infertility clinic provides a money-back guarantee to women who pay its basic price of $12,500.

- A Portland, Oregon, company specializing in menopause products by mail gives free advice from a naturopathic physician on its Internet Web site.

American women have never been reluctant to spend money on health care. They are most likely to buy the family's cough medicine, rush a child to the doctor for stitches, and wait in pediatricians' offices. They are also more likely than men to visit a doctor or hospital. Yet it is only recently that the health-care industry has realized the power of women as health-care consumers. As competition heightens in health care, women have emerged as the most important customers for health products and services—the *grandes dames* of health care.

Thousands of hospital-based women's health-care centers now offer everything from massage therapy to menopause seminars and Internet lessons. A barrage of explicit advertising now promotes women's health products that were once sold almost in secret. And record-breaking sales are registered for drugs such as American Home Product's Premarin, an estrogen replacement product whose sales totaled $854 million in 1994. Health insurers now portray women in their advertising in hopes that women will choose their family's health plans.

Cosmetic companies such as Avon make major contributions to the fight against breast cancer to appeal to their customers.

Marketing health care to women is not easy, because women are a moving target whose needs are always changing. They are increasingly educated, informed, demanding, and hard to please. But the potential rewards are great.

- Women describe themselves as the primary household decision maker about health care in about two-thirds of U.S. households.
- They spend 70 to 80 cents of every dollar that goes to American drugstores.
- They account for 60 percent of all visits to physicians.
- They are more likely than their husbands to choose a family's health-insurance plan.

Physicians and other providers of health care have been influenced by facts like these. "When you're communicating about health care, you have to communicate to women," says George Junginger, a health marketer at the Society of Diagnostic Medical Sonographers. "Everyone carves up who does what in a marriage. Men may keep the checkbook and the car. But when it comes to health-care, women are the ones I want to influence."

Hospitals are listening, too. "We started going into the women's center business [because] women are going to decide who comes to our hospital," says Karen Schuss Rowinsky, who provides educational programming for the women's center at Stormont-Vail Regional Center in Topeka, Kansas.

Choosing the right appeal to American women is treacherous. Women aged 18 and older are a huge group of 102 million whose needs are varied and constantly changing. The woman who is interested in birth services in 1997 probably won't care about a hospital's birthing rooms by 2007. By 2027, she may choose a hospital for its diabetes care program. Her passage through life changes a woman's concerns from contraception to childbirth, motherhood, children's health, menopause, arthritis, and other issues.

Women's health marketers face a group whose members range from teenagers deciding what type of tampon to use to octogenarians wondering whether continued osteoporosis testing is worth the trouble. And women's attitudes toward health vary dramatically by age. Many older women are reluctant to challenge their doctors and embarrassed to discuss certain health problems, but younger women are coming of age in an era when intimate sexual matters are discussed openly on television. The most challenging group may be baby-boom women, who were told in the 1960s and 1970s that learning about their conditions and questioning doctors are acts of medical liberation.

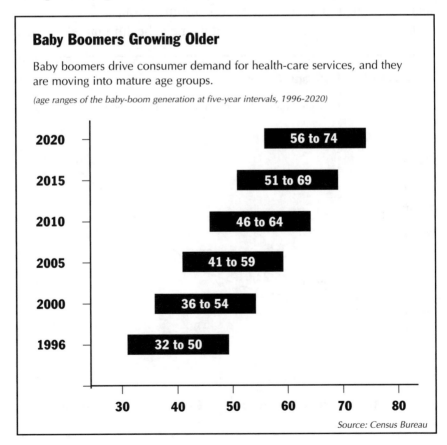

Baby Boomers Growing Older

Baby boomers drive consumer demand for health-care services, and they are moving into mature age groups.

(age ranges of the baby-boom generation at five-year intervals, 1996-2020)

2020	56 to 74
2015	51 to 69
2010	46 to 64
2005	41 to 59
2000	36 to 54
1996	32 to 50

Source: Census Bureau

Sending a single message to a market this large is hazardous. Is child-birth a women's issue? Not for a woman over 70, or a happily childless 35-year-old. "I tell people all the time, only 7 out of 100 women of child-bearing age give birth every year," says Sally Rynne, a women's health marketer in Evanston, Illinois. Savvy health marketers know how to segment their audience and how to approach them so their message is heard.

But how should you divide the women's market? Are there products and services in health care that appeal to all women? What, if anything, unites women as a market? Confusion about these questions has spawned a vigorous industry of women's health consultants and experts in women's health marketing. They have found that the women's market is both a singular and diverse consumer group.

Decades of experience have taught women's health marketers what

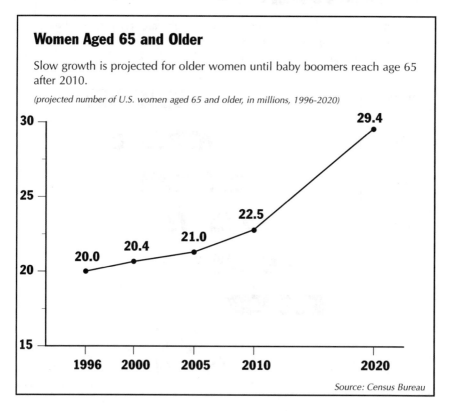

Women Aged 65 and Older

Slow growth is projected for older women until baby boomers reach age 65 after 2010.

(projected number of U.S. women aged 65 and older, in millions, 1996-2020)

Source: Census Bureau

works and does not work in their field. They describe a market with hundreds of overlapping segments. Moreover, the market will change as the structure of the U.S. population changes.

Generations in Transition

In the 1990s, the largest generation of U.S. women are members of the baby-boom generation. The oldest baby boomer turned 50 in 1996, while the youngest turned 32. Because the baby boom is so large, their aging will have a tremendous impact on the U.S. population.

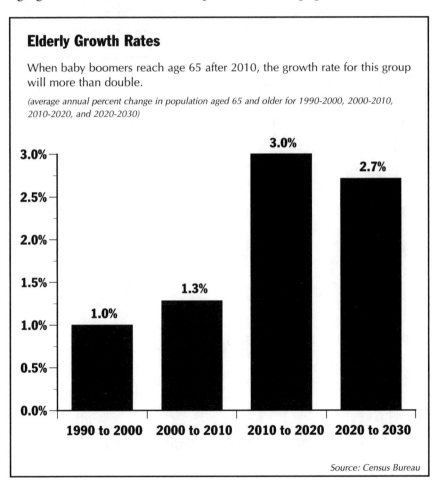

Elderly Growth Rates

When baby boomers reach age 65 after 2010, the growth rate for this group will more than double.

(average annual percent change in population aged 65 and older for 1990-2000, 2000-2010, 2010-2020, and 2020-2030)

Source: Census Bureau

The women's market for health care will also be profoundly affected by the aging of the baby boomers. Every life event that is currently used as a marketing focus, from childbirth to menopause, will change in importance as boomers push up the median age of the population. Moreover, the aging of women will have a dramatic effect on the size and composition of different patient groups. Many common health conditions linked to age are more likely to occur among women than among men. The number of women aged 15 and older with arthritis, for example, is expected to increase from 23 million in 1989-91 to 36 million in 2020.

Some life events, such as childbirth, may become less important to health marketers because the number of women having babies is not

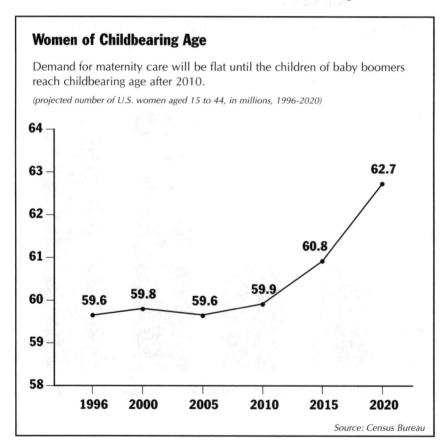

Women of Childbearing Age

Demand for maternity care will be flat until the children of baby boomers reach childbearing age after 2010.

(projected number of U.S. women aged 15 to 44, in millions, 1996-2020)

Source: Census Bureau

expected to grow. The share of the U. S. population comprised of women aged 15 to 44 is expected to remain stable at 22 percent from 1996 to 2000 and drop to 19 percent by 2020. The Census Bureau also projects that the birth rate will drop lower than ever before by 2005, due to smaller numbers of fertile women.

The relative scarcity of younger women doesn't mean that childbirth products and services will no longer be profitable. But in most areas, providers of childbirth products and services need to plan for decades of limited growth and more intense competition.

Age groups are only one way to define Americans, and many other population differences will also shape the future of the women's health market. What role will affluent and more educated women play in the changing health marketplace? How will the increasing number and percentage of minority women affect sales and marketing of health products? Will regional differences in birth rates and age structure make a difference in health marketing trends? The answers to these and other questions will dictate the successful tactics health-care providers use when they approach women.

Successfully marketing to women will require more than simply knowing about the product, the price, and the demographics. Women's lives have changed radically over the last two decades. Just as they have redefined motherhood, marriage, and the workplace, women have also redefined their tastes in health care. Only by listening can providers determine what women want out of health-care today and how to meet their needs tomorrow.

From Potions to Protest

How did women become gatekeepers of the family's health? The answer lies as far back as the Middle Ages, when women crafted their own medicine, and as recently as the 1970s, when the women's health movement lashed out at the medical establishment.

Women were the household health experts well before the era of antibiotics and advertising. Although they were banned from most medical schools in the Middle Ages, women were relied upon as mid-wives and village healers. In fact, historians suggest that many of the women killed during Europe's Medieval witch hunts were guilty only of practicing medicine.

In the United States, 19th- and early 20th-century women practiced midwifery and folk medicine, and they were avid readers of family health manuals. Women have always been the natural experts in such areas as menstrual periods, childbearing, and menopause. Men devised a variety of medical solutions to all three problems. But women tradi-tionally took care of "female problems" at home without professional assistance.

In the 1990s, menstruation is a commercial event with wide-scale merchandising of feminine-hygiene products. But it was not always so. Women engineered their own solutions to the menstrual problem using household materials until the 1920s, when sanitary napkins were invented. They were responsible for handling other problems, too. "Wife Takes Full Blame," trumpeted a 1934 ad for Dr. West's Water Proofed Toothbrush. "Entire family had *dull*-white teeth—all using *soggy* toothbrushes that failed to clean."

But women also were glorified for their homemaking and shopping duties. A 1928 ad for an advertising agency called her "The Little Woman, G.P.A.," or "General Purchasing Agent" of the home. "Without elaborate research...these executives spend annually 40 billion dollars," it said. How do they do it? By reading advertisements, of course.

Growing Resistance

The first rumblings of women's resistance to the status quo in health-care came in the late 1940s, when a small movement began challenging the way women gave birth. Women activists encouraged mothers to breast feed and began developing educational materials to show women what childbirth was like. But most members of the medical establish-ment continued to promote bottle feeding and anesthesia during birth throughout the 1950s and much of the 1960s. "It took approximately 30 years...to move education regarding childbirth from the perception that it was a fad promoted by 'fringe' self-educated women," writes midwife Eunice K.M. Ernst.

By the late 1960s, the aggressive promotion of health and other products to women came under broad attack from the burgeoning women's movement. The feminists of the 1960s drew attention to concerns that still resonate in the marketplace. A key focus was the way women's health services and products are sold, promoted, and distributed to women. Critics charged that health-care advertising was demeaning to women, that the medical profession should open its ranks to female doctors, and that medical care for women should be changed.

The book *Our Bodies, Ourselves*, published in 1969 by the Boston Women's Health Book Collective, was a manual for women taking charge of their own health. The book helped provide a focus for baby-boom women who wanted to learn about their bodies and how to take care of themselves.

A 1977 book called *Seizing Our Bodies* shows how the anger of the 1970s foreshadowed what health consumers would want in the 1990s. "All Americans suffer from the organization of the medical system, but women, by virtue of their reproductive systems, suffer more," it says. "Obstetrics-gynecology is staffed by a physician population that is 93 percent male. Nearly every American woman must deal with a masculine point of view at the most crucial periods of her life: when she needs contraception, when she gives birth, when she enters menopause, more often than not she confronts a system of thought that encourages her to think of normal functions as illness."

By the 1970s, health care began changing in response to its many dissatisfied customers. One change was greater encouragement to women applying to medical schools. In 1993, women made up 26 percent of obstetrician-gynecologists, according to the American College of Obstetrician Gynecologists (ACOG). In 1994, obstetrics-gynecology women outnumbered men among residents. But the widespread concern that women are not receiving the types of services they want remains a driving force in health care.

"The women's health movement has been the primary engine that has driven every expression of interest on women's health," says Leslie Wolfe, president of the Center for Women Policy Studies in Washington, D.C. "The most powerful thing is the idea that women must have control and knowledge."

Businesses quickly saw the financial rewards in catering to the women's health movement. Health-care firms began selling products that had only been available from doctors, such as home pregnancy tests and medication for yeast infections. Such products serve a willing, well-educated group of women who are eager to manage their own health.

Women's health centers and freestanding birth centers are also cre-

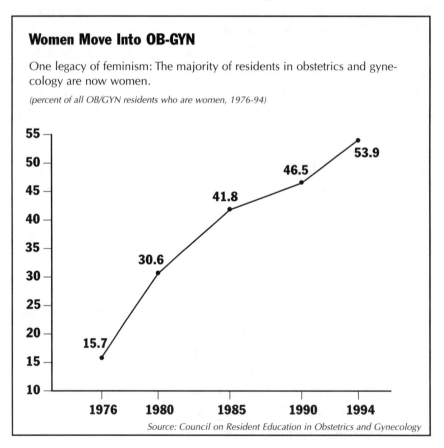

Women Move Into OB-GYN

One legacy of feminism: The majority of residents in obstetrics and gynecology are now women.

(percent of all OB/GYN residents who are women, 1976-94)

Source: Council on Resident Education in Obstetrics and Gynecology

ations of the women's health movement. In 1992, nearly one in four hospitals had a women's health center. In 1995, there were 3,600 women's health centers operating in and out of U.S. hospitals.

Pharmaceutical companies have focused on the special needs of women for decades. But the women's movement also affected the way drug companies market to women, and drug companies now strive to please a more critical, better-informed female consumer.

One focus of women's anger was the drug DES, a synthetic estrogen prescribed widely to American women to prevent miscarriages from the late 1940s to the early 1970s. In 1971, just when the women's health movement was gaining momentum, researchers discovered that DES caused a rare form of cancer in a small number of daughters of women who had taken the drug. The drug had been marketed aggressively to physicians and promoted as safe and effective.

The outcry against drug companies and the marketers who promoted DES was one of several events in the 1970s to put a negative focus on pharmaceutical promotion methods. The Dalkon Shield, a contraceptive device, also was pulled from the market after it was discovered to cause infection leading to infertility and other health problems in some women users.

Many young women today have never heard of DES, the Dalkon Shield, or the women who criticized organized medicine for its support of these products. But the emerging generation of women health consumers has inherited many of their older sisters' ideas about taking charge of their own health care. Like the boomers, younger women are likely to speak up when they don't like the health care they receive.

A Particular Consumer

Women's willingness to speak up about health-care problems is one of eight key differences between the women's health market and the men's market for health care. Compared with men, women are:

- More likely to be dissatisfied with health care.

- More likely to seek information about health problems.
- More likely to be frustrated about the way doctors talk to them.
- Older, because women live an average of seven years longer than men.
- More frequent visitors to doctors and hospitals.
- More pressed for time.
- More likely to make family health decisions.
- More concerned about women's health processes such as menstruation, childbirth, and menopause.

Women's willingness to criticize health providers is well documented. In 1993, a Commonwealth Fund survey of 2,500 American women found that 41 percent had changed physicians at some time because they were dissatisfied, compared with 27 percent of the 1,000 men surveyed. "Women are increasingly knowledgeable [about health] and have much more self confidence," says Maxine F. Brinkman, director of women's and children's services for North Iowa Mercy Health Center in Mason City, Iowa. "It used to be that women thought that the world would cave in if they left a physician practice. They didn't do it. Today, women look at health care as something to be purchased."

Women's dissatisfaction is also related to the differing ways women and men communicate with physicians. The leading reason for a woman to change doctors is communication problems, according to the Commonwealth survey. One in four women reported that they had been "talked down to" or treated like a child by their physician. Only 12 percent of men reported they were treated this way.

Other communication problems emerged in a study of 800 women and 200 men by the Center for Women Policy Studies in 1994. One-third of women said their doctors "decide what is wrong without really listening," and 21 percent of women feared that their doctor would trivialize their problem.

The importance of good communication between doctors and women is a constant thread in these surveys. That's because women value relationships in medicine in ways many men do not, according to women who market and provide health services. For example, the 1994 study found that women were more likely than men to value having their doctor listen to them. Ninety-three percent of women agreed that a doctor should listen to you, while 80 percent of men agreed. Women appear to care more about having an attentive doctor because they don't take this for granted, says Wolfe. "A lot of men assume they are equal [to their physician]. They assume they will be treated with respect."

Communication problems between women and their doctors may stem in part from the different communication styles of men and women. Four out of five physicians were men in 1994. The differences

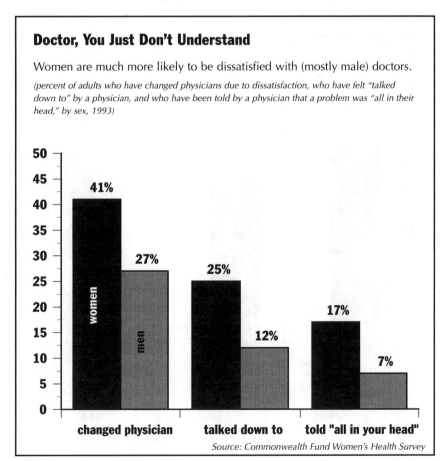

Doctor, You Just Don't Understand

Women are much more likely to be dissatisfied with (mostly male) doctors.

(percent of adults who have changed physicians due to dissatisfaction, who have felt "talked down to" by a physician, and who have been told by a physician that a problem was "all in their head," by sex, 1993)

Source: Commonwealth Fund Women's Health Survey

between the way men and women communicate in everyday life has been explored extensively by popular authors such as Deborah Tannen, author of the book *You Just Don't Understand*.

But women's frustration over the way physicians communicate may also stem from their higher expectations. Researcher Sherrie Kaplan, Ph.D., has found that a woman's average encounter with a doctor often reflects the greater experience she has in medical matters compared with men. When women and men view the same videotape of a doctor talking to a patient, women are more critical than men. Women ask doctors more questions than men do, says Kaplan, a public health expert and co-director of the Primary Care Outcomes Research

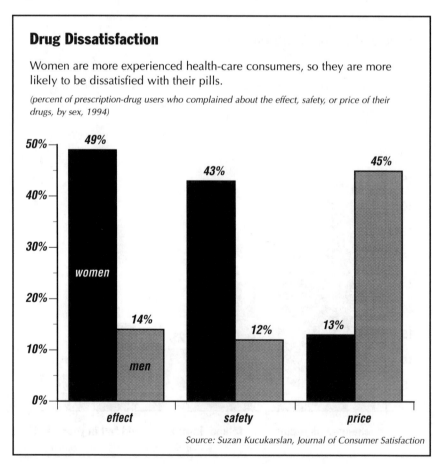

Drug Dissatisfaction

Women are more experienced health-care consumers, so they are more likely to be dissatisfied with their pills.

(percent of prescription-drug users who complained about the effect, safety, or price of their drugs, by sex, 1994)

Source: Suzan Kucukarslan, *Journal of Consumer Satisfaction*

Institute at New England Medical Center. Moreover, "women ask better questions. They ask more active questions," she says.

Kaplan analyzed the way several thousand patients acted during office visits with physicians. A large majority of men did not ask any questions during a 15-minute office visit. Women asked an average of six questions, and very few women had no questions. Women simply have higher standards for physician behavior, says Kaplan.

Women are also more demanding customers at the drug counter. They are far more likely than men to complain about the effectiveness or safety of a pharmaceutical product, according to a 1994 study by Suzan N. Kucukarslan, Ph.D., assistant professor in the College of Pharmacy at Ohio State University.

Of 277 people receiving prescription drugs for the first time, one in five complained about its effectiveness. Eighty-two percent of these dissatisfied users were women. Most of the complainers spoke to the physician who prescribed the drug, though some complained to the pharmacist or the manufacturer.

The survey could indicate that women expect drugs to be more effective than they really are, says Kucukarslan. If so, the information provided to them from their doctors could be more hype than truth. Manufacturers may be setting themselves up for complaints by making ambitious claims for their products. She suggests investing in more information for patients and making sure they learn more about the product before they use it.

Don't Waste Their Time

Women's strong desire for information about health products and services has created a nationwide industry in newsletters, pamphlets, and seminars from women's health centers, drug companies, and physicians. "Women are education-seeking objects," says Mary Anne Graf, a health-care consultant and president of Health Care Innovations, Inc., a market research group in Salt Lake City, Utah. When Sandoz Pharmaceutical Corporation (now Novartis) introduced Miacalcin nasal spray in 1995, up to 800 women at a time attended the company's seminars about this new treatment for osteoporosis.

Women depend on magazine articles and other print media for personal health information, according to the Center for Women Policy Studies. While women in their survey were most likely to say they trusted their physicians for health information, 52 percent said they also depended on women's magazines as sources of information.

This hunger for knowledge reflects differences in men's and women's attitudes about health, says Lois Green, a health-care consultant in Canoga Park, California. "Women are more open to receiving [health] information. Men generally don't seek it out from outside sources. Men traditionally are not comfortable admitting they don't know something, or even dealing with their own illnesses."

Indeed, researchers have found that men are more likely than women to ignore certain health problems. Women are more likely than men to talk to a doctor about chest pains, and more likely to cut down their activities when they are sick.

Not all women have the time, interest, or money to buy magazines and books about health, or to hear seminars about the newest drugs. Women with higher levels of education are much more likely than women with lower levels of education to seek out such information. This is true even though less-educated women, who are more likely to be poor than better-educated women, would often benefit the most from health information.

Low-income women are less likely to be screened for disease and more likely than other women to die from diabetes. They also are more likely to discover cancer when it is well-established and less likely to be treated successfully. The 1993 Commonwealth Fund Women's Health Survey found that 62 percent of women aged 50 and older who had a college degree or more had received a mammogram within the past year, compared with 43 percent of women the same ages who had less than a high school diploma.

Yet there is no evidence that women with low education levels are less interested in their health. Indeed, the popularity of services such as the counseling and brochures offered by Planned Parenthood, which serves women of all income levels, suggest that women at all educational levels want to learn more about health care.

As childbearers, primary child-care providers, and the sex likely to live longest, women spend more time at the doctor's office. They develop a keen knowledge of what good health care looks like, and they know when things are going wrong. American women made an average of 3.5 visits to the doctor in 1992, compared with 2.5 visits made by men. Women also spent more time as patients in the hospital. A total of 12.5 out of every 100 women were discharged from a hospital after a short stay in 1991, compared with 9 out of every 100 men. And women spend even more time at the offices of pediatricians and others who care for their children. Though 79 percent of married women aged 35 to 44 were members of the work force in 1992, mothers still are more likely than fathers to take children to the doctor. Children under age 5 visited the doctor an average of 7 times in 1993. A woman with two small children might take them to the doctor 14 times a year.

All that waiting-room time educates women about the system. "If practice doesn't make perfect, it certainly makes it easier," says Kaplan. Men might face their first health crisis in their 50s. By that age, most women have already learned what they want from a physician and how they want to receive it.

Women dislike waiting for care, and their aversion appears to have intensified over the years. In 1960, when 37 percent of married women aged 35 to 44 were in the work force, a long wait at the doctor's office may have rankled. But surveys suggest that now all Americans—and particularly working mothers—are pressed for time. In 1992, 38 percent of Americans said they "always felt rushed," compared with 32 percent in 1985 and 22 percent in 1971, according to the 1992 National Recreation and Park Association Survey and the 1985 Americans' Use of Time Project. Working mothers are the most rushed of the bunch: in 1992, 64 percent said they always felt rushed, compared with 57 percent for working fathers.

For health marketers, this is a clear signal that women will respond to time-saving opportunities. "Time is a major issue for women," says Kathleen L. Lewton, a senior vice president for Porter/Novelli in Chicago and the author of *Public Relations in Health Care: A Guide for Professionals.* "Whether they are in the home or working outside the home, there's a time issue. We tell doctors that evening and Saturday hours are essential."

Sixty percent of the more than 40,000 women she has interviewed prefer office hours in the evening, according to Ruthie H. Dearing, co-author of the 1987 book *Marketing Women's Health Care* and president of Dearing and Associates in Spokane. Yet only about 20 to 30 percent of American doctors had evening office hours in 1996. In areas where doctors begin offering these services, others quickly follow suit to become more competitive. "The doctors who are busiest and most successful are doing it," says Dearing. "They are doing what it takes to be busy five years from now."

Richer and Bigger

Despite their primary importance as health-care consumers, the special needs of women continue to be ignored by many health-care executives. The continuing problems in the industry range from the way physicians communicate with women to the way insurers challenge funding for services many women see as essential, such as osteoporosis testing. Yet the importance of women to health care is great today and will be greater tomorrow.

The huge influx of women into the work force over the last 20 years means that women are now more likely to earn their own money, and to earn a good wage if they are working. The proportion of women aged 16 and older who are in the work force increased from an average of 43 percent in 1970 to 59 percent in 1994. And working women's average full-time incomes increased from a median of $223 a week in 1980 ($391.50 in inflation adjusted 1993 dollars) to $432 in 1993.

Younger and middle-aged women who are in the work force are also likely to be developing their own pensions. As these women age, they will transform the economic profile of older women in America. Older women may continue to have less money than older men. But in the future, they will be far more likely to have their own disposable income and assets to spend on health products, health services, and supplementary health insurance.

The growth of managed care has also amplified the importance of marketing to women. Smart hospitals and physicians must find ways to show women that their services are worth choosing when they select a managed-care plan. This means devising ways to stay in the public's eye.

Changing public standards have also made marketing to women more important. Readers of contemporary magazines, where advertisements for everything from estrogen supplements to condoms are routine, may forget that as recently as the early 1980s pharmaceutical companies advertised prescription products exclusively to doctors.

When drug companies began advertising directly to consumers in the middle 1980s, the market for women's drugs changed. Between 1990 and 1994, total consumer advertising of prescription products increased from $48 million to $187 million, according to Competitive Media Reporting. This includes massive marketing of women's drugs such as Premarin estrogen supplements and Depo-Provera birth control. By advertising directly to users, drug companies offer women yet another way to feel that they are taking charge of their health care.

While advertisements for women's products have become more graphic, television networks continue to censor some messages. This continuing ban shows that some women's health products are still seen as unacceptable for public viewing.

"We've broken down a lot of barriers," says Janey Loyd, vice president for business development at Tambrands in White Plains, New York. "A few years ago, you could not say the word 'period'. Now you can. You couldn't show a tampon applicator, but you could show a woman running through a field of flowers. Now you can show an applicator." Yet tampons still cannot be shown on television, even as talk shows discuss women sleeping with their children's babysitters and the topic of transsexuality.

The distance from a field of flowers to an image of a tampon applicator is the difference between romance and real life. This difference continues to challenge those who provide health care to women. Many health marketers continue to depict romantic or flower-strewn landscapes when selling products and services to women. Others depend on less prosaic factors such as price and the way a product works.

Either approach might succeed for some products, segments of women, and in selective markets. Knowing as much as possible about women as health consumers is the best way to navigate this dynamic market.

Chapter 2

The Future of Childbirth

P icture a bridal show in Atlanta that is teeming with brides-to-be, their anxious mothers, and dreamy younger sisters. You're approaching a booth that has a small television perched on a table. You have already seen videotapes hawking silver services and honeymoon resorts playing in the exhibit hall, but this one is different. Moving closer, you're transfixed by the screen.

It's a live birth. The booth is sponsored by Atlanta Women's Specialists, a group of doctors and midwives who want your business after the honeymoon.

Welcome to the anything-but-squeamish new world of marketing childbirth services. Not long ago, most things having to do with childbirth were only discussed in private. Today, talk of childbirth is so much an element of public life that fashionable southern brides gravitate to films of the process.

Maternity specialists now sell products and services of reproduction and childbirth to working women who tend to be demanding, intelligent customers. Sales in this most womanly category have increased dramatically over the last decade, as the huge baby-boom generation has moved through its child-bearing years. Oral contraceptives were a $930 million market in 1990; 1995 sales are estimated at $1.5 billion by the research firm FIND/SVP. Retail sales of feminine-hygiene products in the U.S. have increased from $1.5 billion in 1989 to $1.8 billion in 1993, according to Packaged Facts.

But now the market is changing. As the first baby-boom women reach their 50th birthdays and enter menopause, childbirth marketers may find it necessary to take more aggressive approaches to maintain sales growth. The Atlanta Women's Services booth is an example of this new, more direct approach.

The movie goes from showing the live birth to scenes of the practice, and of the doctors and midwives at work. "It's intriguing," says Lisa Borders Marbury, administrator for the practice. "It just draws people in. After a trade show, we get 20 to 30 patients in the next month."

Efforts like Marbury's are not traditional and perhaps not suited to other markets. "We're not leading edge, we're bleeding edge," she says proudly. But most organizations that sell health services to young women will have to adopt more aggressive strategies as their patient base changes in the next decade. The changes include:

- *Fewer new moms.* Most U.S. markets will see slow growth in the

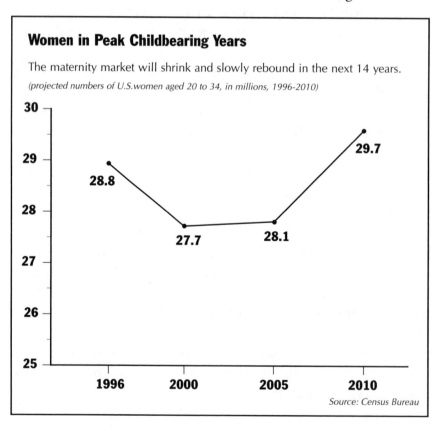

Women in Peak Childbearing Years

The maternity market will shrink and slowly rebound in the next 14 years.

(projected numbers of U.S. women aged 20 to 34, in millions, 1996-2010)

28.8

27.7

28.1

29.7

1996   2000   2005   2010

Source: Census Bureau

number of women of childbearing age, along with a declining number of women in the peak years for childbearing. The overall market—the number of U.S. women aged 15 to 44—will increase from about 59 million in 1990 to 60 million in 2000, then remain unchanged until 2005. Yet the number of women in their peak childbearing ages, 20 to 34, is predicted to fall from 31 million in 1995 to 28 million in 2000 and 2005. Women aged 20 to 34 will not rebound to their 1995 level until after the year 2015, according to Census Bureau projections.

- *Regional differences.* While the national trend is for slow growth or stagnation, the number of births in some markets will continue to grow rapidly while others see absolute declines. The Northeast and the Midwest are expected to see their population of 18-to-44 year-old women drop steadily until the year 2010, but western states should see a steady increase in this group. Southern states are expected to see their population of women aged 18 to 44 increase until the year 2000, then decrease back to 1995 levels in 2010. Birth rates are also expected to vary by region. As a result, hospitals could see increasing numbers of babies if they are in a market where the population is younger than average or includes a high share of racial or ethnic minorities. Utah had the nation's highest birth rate in 1994, with 20.1 babies born for every 1,000 residents. Maine had the lowest birth rate, with 11.6 per 1,000.

- *Fewer babies.* The annual number of births in the U.S. exceeded 4 million between 1989 and 1993, but it dropped just below 4 million in 1994 and is not expected to break that mark again until the year 2008. After 2008, births will rise again as the 69 million children of baby boomers, born between 1977 and 1994, begin having children themselves. In the year 2018, births are projected to exceed 4.5 million.

The birth rate is also expected to fall through the late 1990s. Birth rates hit a postwar peak in 1957, when 25.3 babies were born for

States of Birth

Fast-growing and southern states have the highest birth rates; slow-growing and northern states have the lowest.

(top- and bottom-ten states for birth rate per 1,000 residents, 1994)

Top Ten

Rank	State	Birth rate
1	Utah	20.1
2	California	18.1
3	Alaska	17.6
4	Texas	17.5
5	Arizona	17.4
6	New Mexico	16.7
7	Hawaii	16.6
8	Nevada	16.4
9	Illinois	16.1
10	Georgia	15.7
	Louisiana	15.7
	Mississippi	15.7
	United States	**15.5**

Bottom Ten

Rank	State	Birth rate
40	North Dakota	13.5
41	Rhode Island	13.5
42	Wyoming	13.5
43	Wisconsin	13.4
44	New Hampshire	13.3
45	Iowa	13.1
46	Pennsylvania	13.0
47	Montana	12.9
48	Vermont	12.7
49	West Virginia	11.7
50	Maine	11.6

Source: National Center for Health Statistics

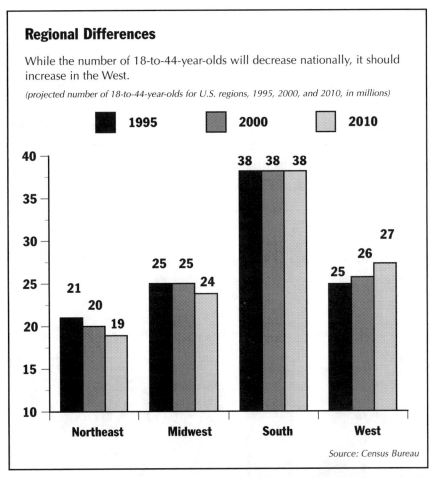

Regional Differences

While the number of 18-to-44-year-olds will decrease nationally, it should increase in the West.

(projected number of 18-to-44-year-olds for U.S. regions, 1995, 2000, and 2010, in millions)

■ **1995**   ▨ **2000**   □ **2010**

Source: Census Bureau

every 1,000 people in the population. But decline has been fairly steady since then, with a brief upswing from 1988 to 1991. The rate stood at about 15.6 in 1995, and the Census Bureau expects it to sink to a record low of 13.9 in 2026. Fewer children and a lower birth rate means more than just a tougher market for hospitals. It means fewer customers for childbirth-related products, including drugs used in labor and delivery, products to help breast-feeding mothers, baby formula, and diapers.

- *More minority mothers.* Higher birth rates among Hispanics, blacks, and some other groups will run counter to a national slowdown in births among non-Hispanic whites. The number of children born to minority women is often higher than it is for non-Hispanic white women, but this isn't the only reason for the minority baby boom. Hispanic- and Asian-American immigrants are highly likely to be young adults in the midst of their childbearing years.

Hispanic birth rates, at 25.5 per 1,000 people, were higher in 1994 than the national birth rate was in 1957. Hispanics were about 16 percent of U.S. births in 1995, and are expected to make up 17.5 percent by the year 2000 and 19 percent by 2005. In many southern

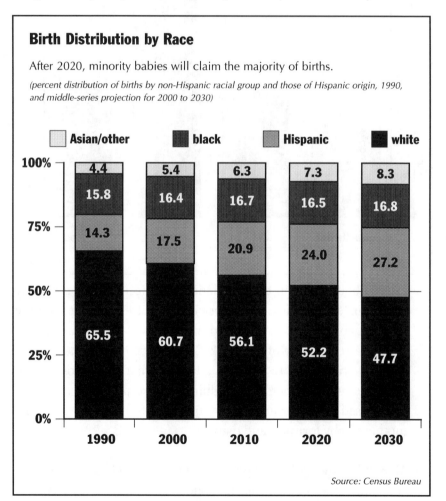

Birth Distribution by Race

After 2020, minority babies will claim the majority of births.

(percent distribution of births by non-Hispanic racial group and those of Hispanic origin, 1990, and middle-series projection for 2000 to 2030)

Asian/other   black   Hispanic   white

	1990	2000	2010	2020	2030
Asian/other	4.4	5.4	6.3	7.3	8.3
black	15.8	16.4	16.7	16.5	16.8
Hispanic	14.3	17.5	20.9	24.0	27.2
white	65.5	60.7	56.1	52.2	47.7

Source: Census Bureau

and western states, Hispanic women will approach or exceed a majority of births.

Births to Asians are also expected to continue climbing. Asians were slightly more than 4 percent of U.S. births in 1995; they are expected to make up 5 percent in 2000 and 6.3 percent in 2005. In California and some large urban markets, their share is far greater.

Blacks also are predicted to maintain above-average birth rates. But the Census Bureau predicts that black birth rates will decline in the future, mainly because this group has not been absorbing large numbers of young adults from other countries. In 1994, blacks had 19.5 births per 1,000 people, compared with 14.9 per 1,000 whites.

The declining white birth rate, and the growing number of births to racial and ethnic minorities, mean that multicultural marketing will be increasingly important to the success of childbirth products and services. Some maternity centers in the U.S. are placing Spanish-language advertising on radio and TV, and marketers of childbirth products are also placing ads in local and national publications for black Americans. The 1995 campaign for the contraceptive Depo-Provera, for example, included many magazines with heavy black readership.

- *Bye-bye to boomers.* The last woman of the baby-boom generation will give birth in about 2014, when she turns 50. Until then, baby boomers will steadily cede the childbearing world to the smaller generation of 44 million Americans born between 1965 and 1976. Marketers must be attuned to the different values of mothers who belong to this generation, often called the "baby bust" because of its relatively small size.

One way to look at these values is to consider what demographers call the "cohort effect," or the traits that develop in groups according to influences during the formative years of 17 to 21. Baby-boom women came of age during the heyday of the women's health movement, when young people were encouraged to question authority. They saw the birth of the modern environmental movement, with its emphasis on "natural" products. The popularity of patient-controlled health products and services such as home pregnancy tests and "natural" childbirth is no coincidence.

Baby-bust women matured at a time when the "natural" label could be found on everything from clothing to candy, so they may not attach as much significance to the term—or they may take it for granted. They were more likely to be treated by women physicians, and more likely to be raised by working mothers, than were baby boomers. The decreasing demand for "natural" childbirth and the growing interest in using

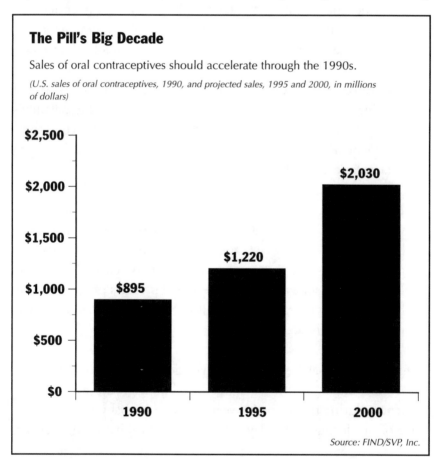

The Pill's Big Decade

Sales of oral contraceptives should accelerate through the 1990s.

(U.S. sales of oral contraceptives, 1990, and projected sales, 1995 and 2000, in millions of dollars)

Source: FIND/SVP, Inc.

female obstetrician-gynecologists for prenatal care stems largely from the baby bust's preferences.

The challenge for childbirth marketers is to serve both generations until about 2005, then craft new messages for the huge generation of baby boomers' children. The 69 million-member generation known as the "echo boom" or "the next baby boom" is aged 2 to 19 in 1996, and this group will dominate the childbearing market in the first decade of the 21st century. The news events and cultural trends of 1995 to 2005 will help determine the values and attitudes of this generation throughout their lives.

The population trends that affect childbearing are complex, and some trends that bode well for one product type may be bad news for another. For example, a falling birth rate that makes hospitals earn less money could also mean bigger profits for contraceptive manufacturers.

Factors that go beyond population change have also kept birth-related products in flux over the last few decades. Changes in contraceptive technology, revelations about health hazards linked to tampons and birth-control pills, and shifting attitudes about the role of mothers in birth have shaped the market at least as significantly as have population changes. These social and technological changes vary industry by industry, and they will play a key role in shaping the future.

Childbirth Meets Managed Care

Hospitals generally don't give anything away. But in late 1995, Tampa General Health Care announced it would be cutting the price of its rooms from over $200 per night to zero. Any woman who had given birth in the hospital would be eligible to stay for free at the hospital for the next 48 hours after their medical discharge.

Tampa General's gamble started after Fred Karl, the retired chief executive officer and a father of seven, decided that something had to be done for women like his youngest daughter. She gave birth at another hospital and was sent home after 12 hours. "She was a wreck," says

Claudia Mahoney, director of women's and children's services at the hospital. Karl's announcement galvanized interest in the hospital, triggering media coverage and a swell of customer interest. "It ended up being a good marketing plan, but I don't think that was the idea," says Mahoney.

Tampa General loses money on the extra night's stay. But its willingness to launch the program is a measure of the importance of childbirth services to hospitals. Childbirth is a steadily lucrative procedure that provides bread-and-butter income and future patient loyalty. Thirty-

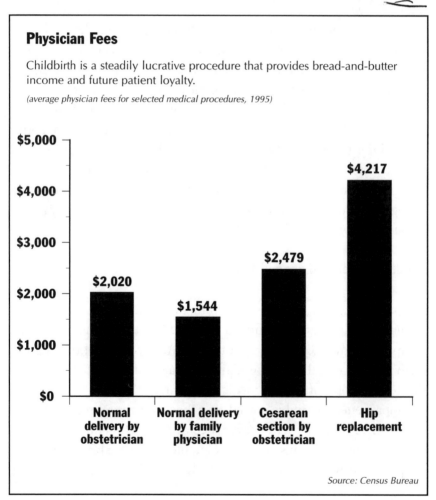

Physician Fees

Childbirth is a steadily lucrative procedure that provides bread-and-butter income and future patient loyalty.

(average physician fees for selected medical procedures, 1995)

- $2,020 — Normal delivery by obstetrician
- $1,544 — Normal delivery by family physician
- $2,479 — Cesarean section by obstetrician
- $4,217 — Hip replacement

Source: Census Bureau

eight percent of all hospital patients have their first relationship with a hospital through childbirth services, says consultant Ruthie H. Dearing, president of Dearing and Associates in Spokane, Washington.

Obstetrician-gynecologists and family practicioners see childbirth as nine months of steady visits that can be the introduction to a lifelong relationship with a family. Among midwives, childbirth is the only source of business and referrals. And hospitals see it as a crucial opportunity to make a good first impression.

Pregnant women are a prize for health-care providers, and competition for them has intensified with the rise of health maintenance organizations (HMOs) and other managed-health-care plans. Hospitals across the country have opened new maternity units so they can compete with other hospitals for managed-care contracts. Knowing what pregnant women want out of childbirth services gives some of the competitors a powerful advantage.

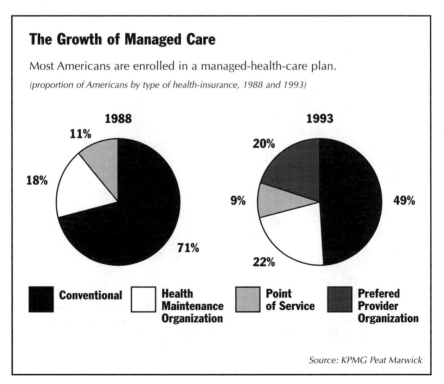

The Growth of Managed Care

Most Americans are enrolled in a managed-health-care plan.

(proportion of Americans by type of health-insurance, 1988 and 1993)

1988
11%
18%
71%

1993
20%
9%
49%
22%

- ■ Conventional
- □ Health Maintenance Organization
- ▨ Point of Service
- ▨ Prefered Provider Organization

Source: KPMG Peat Marwick

The maternity experience has changed drastically in the last decade. During the 1980s, childbirth marketers promoted everything from steak dinners and champagne for new parents to family birthing rooms. "Hospitals were hurtling along," says Kris Powell, director of community health partnerships for Anne Arundel Medical Center in Annapolis, Maryland. "Everybody got champagne, whether or not they wanted champagne." Today, new kinds of approaches are required for mothers who are more demographically diverse, less interested in frills, and more interested in receiving high-quality care at a low price.

The rules of managed-care plans are having a powerful and growing effect on childbirth services. Managed care can dictate how and when

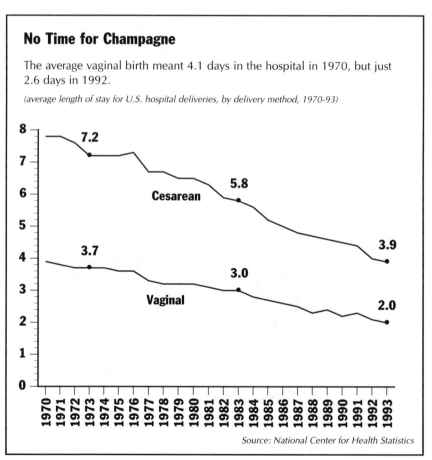

No Time for Champagne

The average vaginal birth meant 4.1 days in the hospital in 1970, but just 2.6 days in 1992.

(average length of stay for U.S. hospital deliveries, by delivery method, 1970-93)

Source: National Center for Health Statistics

women choose their physicians and midwives, what hospitals they use, and how long they stay at the hospital.

In 1988, about 29 percent of Americans with private health insurance were enrolled in managed-care plans. By 1993, 51 percent of Americans with private health insurance were enrolled in managed care, and the proportion continues to grow. One result has been a sharp decrease in the average hospital stay for maternity, from 4.1 days for vaginal birth in 1970 to 2.6 days in 1992. With managed care, most women are no longer at a hospital long enough to enjoy champagne and steak dinners. Health providers in this environment must walk a tightrope, appealing to a more discriminating clientele while keeping costs down.

In the 1980s, hospitals in most markets promoted their services so women would choose them or a doctor affiliated with them after they became pregnant. Today, hospitals in managed care markets must appeal to women when they are choosing their managed-care plan. This choice is often made well before they become pregnant.

For hospitals, knowing the nature of the local health-insurance market is essential. "If you're in a rural area unlikely to get hit by managed care, traditional marketing will work fine," says Mary Anne Graf, of Healthcare Innovations, Inc. "If you're in an area where managed care is established," she says, "it does you no good to market in the traditional way."

Managed Care makes it essential for maternity marketers to give women a positive feeling about their hospital before pregnancy begins. "Anything that will influence decisions at insurance enrollment helps," says Graf. This makes traditional advertising less important than in the past, while highly targeted media such as billboards and direct mail become more important.

The need to appeal to women early is especially important in childbirth services, because women form general impressions of their local hospitals well before their first bout of morning sickness. And it is especially important for hospitals, because most women (58 percent) choose their hospital first and their physician second, according to consultant Ruthie Dearing. "If you're going to market your hospital, your customer is currently looking in her lover's eyes. She's not pregnant yet," says Sally Rynne, president of Women's Healthcare Consultants in Evanston, Illinois.

Although much has changed in marketing childbirth services to women, many of the basics still apply in every market, whether or not managed care is a factor. Marketers across the country continue to follow three key strategies.

First, they **conduct market research** by holding focus groups and taking surveys of women. This is the most reliable way to track the specific services women want in a specific market. "The [preferences] are different for every area and for every age group," says Maxine F. Brinkman, of North Iowa Mercy Health Center. "We have to listen to our customers."

Second, they **promote educational programs**, including a full range of childbirth classes. "Educational programs bring folks into the system," says Powell of Anne Arundel Medical Center.

Third, they **cultivate public attention** to new programs. "Every time something [we do] is in the news, we book new patients," says Terry Mullady Guymon, manager of women's health services at the Women's Health Center of Christ Hospital and Medical Center in Tinley Park, Illinois.

Relationship Marketing

The most effective hospital programs develop links to women that last for years, or what is sometimes called relationship marketing. This can include everything from educational programs to membership programs, urgent-care services, and children's centers. If a hospital has a reputation as a top birthing hospital, women will choose that hospital.

One innovative program pursues healthy women in San Antonio, Texas. The Methodist Healthcare System offers men and women membership in its WomanPlus program for $10. The program provides discounts at stores and restaurants, offers members the chance to take free health classes, provides free transportation to the hospital, and gives some discounts on hospital services.

When WomanPlus was launched in 1987, Methodist Hospital lagged behind competitors in the childbirth market. Eight years later, the hospital is the top San Antonio provider of childbirth services, says Geoffrey Crabtree, vice president of strategic planning and marketing services. "It gives us a relationship to you," he says. "In building that relationship over a period of time, we hope you'll remember us."

The hospital has used the information from the WomanPlus membership form to compile a massive record of individual health profiles, from which it compiles demographic and lifestyle profiles of its current and likely customers. The database's value goes far beyond childbirth marketing, says Crabtree. For example, Methodist General can now send information by mail to women of menopausal age about services for this group. The women are unlikely to be offended that the hospital has such intimate knowledge of their bodies, because they have knowingly offered the information to the hospital.

The database has also allowed the hospital to cut back on general advertising. "If you knew who was going to buy a particular type of candy bar, wouldn't you want to talk to that person? That's what we're doing," says Crabtree. "Though you start off with a general database, you end up targeting women based on their real needs."

Methodist General's system requires top-of-the-line computer capability. Smaller hospitals and obstetric practices have found lower-tech ways to reach out to potential customers that are also effective. Bellevue Woman's Hospital in Niskayuna, New York also sends educators to junior high schools to give programs on puberty, nutrition, and pregnancy. When the girls' soccer team at the local high school won the state championship, the hospital held a reception and gave the girls warm-up jackets. Support of local girls reminds the community about the hospital and its two freestanding primary care women's health centers.

Many hospitals and medical practices use the mail to distribute women's health newsletters. They send newsletters to former patients and likely future prospects. Some are staff produced. Some depend on consultants like Sally Rynne, who sent out 25 million copies of different hospital newsletters in 1995.

A successful women's health newsletter demands a mix of stories. It must not simply emphasize childbirth, even if attracting patients to give birth at a hospital is the goal, says Rynne. "Our clients say, 'Our primary goal is to get women into the maternity market.'" But it is not effective to market maternity services to a large sampling of women. "You hand women a group of newsletters and they see an article about babies. They say, 'You think this is all we are good for,'" she says.

One common mistake is to assume that every woman wants to have children or will ultimately use a practice or hospital for childbirth. In 1996, only 3.8 million babies were born to the 60 million American women aged 15 to 44. "Women start to resent being called baby machines," says Rynne.

One way to reach out to women through the mail is aggressive promotion of educational programs, including programs geared to young couples. A course called "Maybe Baby" is one of dozens offered by Christ Hospital and Medical Center in Oak Lawn, Illinois. The free course examines everything from "preconception planning" to what to expect during pregnancy.

Such courses draw women into the hospital and women's center. They also generate publicity, says Terry Mullady Guymon at the Women's Health Center. "The educational programs have gotten a lot of media attention for us. Sometimes reporters are looking for topics." Guymon allows them virtually unlimited access, including abundant information about women's health topics—even if the story does not feature the hospital.

Attracting Older Mothers

Other hospitals use special kinds of birth education classes to carve out a market niche in the diverse population of pregnant women. Anne Arundel Medical Center offers a birth preparation class for women aged 35 and older that caters to the increasing willingness of American women to delay childbirth. The number of American women giving birth at ages 35 to 39 more than doubled between 1980 and 1994, and the experts see no evidence that women will reverse the trend of having children later in life.

"When a woman who's had a career has a class with a 23-year-old couple, she says, 'Wait a minute,'" says Kris Powell of Anne Arundel. The medical center also offers private birth classes and birth classes for adolescent mothers. The youngest pregnant women are distinctly different than older mothers. "They're still uncomfortable talking about sex. They don't like to touch each other [during class]."

Other childbirth courses appeal to busy working women. Bellevue, The Woman's Hospital in Niskayuna offers a Lamaze Weekend Getaway so women and their partners can complete all pre-birth training in one weekend. The weekend takes place at a hotel, where couples have a chance to swim and relax together, says Ann Boeke, director of corporate planning and development for the hospital.

With women spending less time in the hospital after giving birth, some hospitals also offer at-home services after the baby is born. Holy Name Hospital in Teaneck, New Jersey, arranges for a nurse to visit

---

Mom Gets Older

The number of births to women under age 30 declined 10 percent between 1980 and 1994, but births to women aged 30 and older increased 88 percent.

(thousands of U.S. births by age of mother, 1980-94)

	1980	1990	1994
15 to 29	2,887	2,893	2,596
30 to 34	550	886	906
35 to 39	141	318	372
40 to 44	23	50	64
total	3,612	4,158	3,953

Source: National Center for Health Statistics

mother and baby at home within a week of the child's birth. The service, which started in 1993, is billed to insurance companies. If they are not willing to pay, the hospital picks up the tab.

Physician practices also promote their birth services through education programs. Atlanta Women's Specialists offers breast-feeding classes and 24-hour breast-feeding support from a nurse educator on call after a baby is born. The service has given the practice strong word-of-mouth recommendations, says Guymon. "When she offers to help at midnight, that's a convert. That's a raving fan. A raving fan will give you more patients then you can shake a stick at."

The power of word-of-mouth advertising is immense in childbirth services. A survey conducted by the National Association of Childbearing Centers, a professional organization for facilities operated primarily by midwives, found that word-of-mouth is the most common source of patients for its membership.

Free pregnancy testing is another way to draw maternity patients. The Women's Health Center at Christ Hospital sends an announcement to the 40,000 women on its mailing list three or four times a year, when a new obstetrician joins the staff or the hospital has a special offer. Women are offered a free pregnancy test or pap smear if they visit the new physician. The return on such announcements is dramatic. "I average about 400 booked appointments from brand-new people," says Guymon.

High standards

Adding new services may be the way to appeal to new needs among women, but experts warn hospitals to remember the basic appeal of a clean, welcoming, professional atmosphere. Women visit an average of three hospitals when they're trying to decide where to go to give birth, according to the American Hospital Association study. When they drop by, they know what they want to see.

"Women tend to make a decision in the first four minutes about the quality of a place, based on appearance," says Ruthie Dearing. "It doesn't have to be pink and ooey gooey, but it needs to be contemporary and state of the art."

Women want an atmosphere that suggests they will be treated like individuals, Dearing says. "One of the things that works is highly personalized care. [Women want] care that is unique and special, and not available down the street." Women also want nurses and staff who seem flexible and welcoming, Dearing says. They are willing to travel to a hospital that appeals to them, even if it is not the one closest to their home.

These wishes often create demand for obstetricians or midwifes who are women, says Cheryl E. Stone, vice president of Rynne Marketing Group. Between 20 and 40 percent of women in Stone's surveys prefer a female obstetrician-gynecologist, and between 25 and 30 percent prefer a nurse midwife. Only 7 to 15 percent of women prefer a man for their obstetrician-gynecologist. "The hospital that can bring in women for obstetrician-gynecologist providers will do better in attracting the market," says Stone.

The same rule applies to other medical practices. Women have become more outspoken about wanting a female doctor or midwife in childbirth, says Marbury of Atlanta Women Specialists. "We were losing business about three or four years ago. We had slots available, but we had male practitioners. People would call and say, 'I want a woman.' I started keeping track of how many patients we were losing." The practice now has six female midwives, three obstetrician-gynecologists who are women, and two obstetrician-gynecologists who are men.

About half the women who come to nurse midwives do so because they want a woman to help them through childbirth, says Deanne Williams of the American College of Nurse-Midwives. Only 1 out of every 100 nurse midwives in the U.S. is a man.

Nurse midwives do not threaten the economic well-being of obstetrician-gynecologists, but they are making an increasing share of the deliveries in the U.S. The percentage of babies delivered by physicians dropped from 98.4 percent in 1975 to 94.2 percent in 1992, while the percentage of births attended in hospitals by nurse midwives climbed from 0.6 percent in 1975 to 4.4 percent in 1992, according to FIND/SVP.

Midwife marketing focuses on providing options and offering a better-quality birth experience. Midwives publicize the lower cesarean section rates for births they attend and emphasize personal attention. "A nurse midwife is going to be with you the whole time, not fly in for the last 10 minutes," says Kimberly Pool, spokeswoman for the American College of Nurse-Midwives.

A service provided by caring female health professionals who spend time with their patients matches women's wants and needs in the 1990s. Midwives also cost less. Promotional material from the National Association of Childbearing Centers reports that the average 24-hour stay at a birth center cost 31 percent less than the average 24-hour stay at a hospital in 1993.

The popularity of midwives is likely to increase as managed care spreads, and as women respond to midwives' message. One sign of this is the heavy dependence on nurse midwives by Kaiser Permanente, the massive health-maintenance organization based in California. More than 90 percent of Kaiser's pregnant patients choose midwives with an obstetrician back-up when given a choice between a midwife and an obstetrician, FIND/ SVP reports. Patients are told that midwives will spend more time with them and see them more frequently than an obstetrician would.

Most American women continue to want some obstetric care. A study conducted by the Ketchum Public Relations Research and Measurement Department for the American College of Nurse-Midwives in 1993 found that 68 percent of the 500 women surveyed would only consider using a nurse midwife if they could have periodic checkups during pregnancy from a licensed obstetrician. This preference may lead to more midwife-obstetrician partnerships in the next decade, as managed care continues to press for cost savings.

A Room of One's Own

For years, childbirth education movements such as Lamaze have promoted the idea of birth as a healthy process that should be removed from operating rooms and other surgical settings. The popularity of single-room maternity units has grown out of this movement, and patients' desires for birth settings that are more wholesome and less "clinical."

Women show a "tremendous preference" for having their labor, delivery, and recovery in one room, says Stone of Rynne Marketing Group. Most hospitals in the U.S. now offer some variation on this, with northeastern hospitals slowest to adapt. Some hospitals move women to another room after the birth, in what is called an LDR arrangement, for labor, delivery, and recovery. Other hospitals enable women to stay in the same room in an arrangement called LDRP, with P standing for post-partum.

Stone said that hospitals with a high volume of deliveries generally can't afford to offer LDRP rooms because each room must have expensive birthing equipment. Another difficulty with LDRP is that not all women like the idea. "In consumer focus groups, women say, 'I really want to go to another room because I don't want to be reminded of the birth,'" Stone says. "Others don't want to hear another woman in labor."

Still, the single-room maternity concept holds great opportunities for added services for patients. Holy Name Hospital in Teaneck, New Jersey offers small refrigerators in all its maternity rooms, for example. "Food is important to women after giving birth," says Stone. The refrigerators allow women to have food available any time of day or night. Other hospitals arrange with restaurants to deliver food to mothers right after delivery.

Families are drawn to the freedom of a single-room maternity unit, says Sally Piscotty of St. Joseph's Healthcare System in Albuquerque. Husbands and children often take advantage of the extra sleeping space in the room, and visitors are allowed at any hour. This is particularly appealing to Hispanics, Piscotty says, because "Hispanics tend to like having their families there." St. Joseph's market is about 55 percent Hispanic.

Dividing the Market

As the Hispanic population grows in the U.S., marketing births to Hispanic women will be increasingly important. St. Joseph's has many bilingual staff members, provides educational materials in Spanish, and promotes its services through advertisements in Hispanic publications and a local Spanish-language television station.

Spanish food is a must. The hospital attempted to have a southern contractor manage the food service briefly, but Mexican-American patients revolted at the sight of grits. Now the menu has returned to southwestern standards like rice and beans.

As the percentage of babies born to minority women increases, marketing to these groups' special needs will become increasingly important. Cost-saving measures are also driving hospitals to craft new ways to offer cost-effective services to low-income women, many of whom are minorities. St. Joseph's in Albuquerque is preparing for a Medicaid managed care program through which poor women will receive managed-health-care services. Hospitals in the network will be paid a fixed amount to serve each patient on Medicaid, which gives them an incentive to keep every patient healthy.

A big problem in childbirth services is getting poor women to seek medical care early in pregnancy. In 1992, 1 in 10 pregnant black or Hispanic pregnant women either had no prenatal care or only had care beginning in their third trimester, compared with 1 in 25 pregnant white women. Insufficient prenatal care means a higher percentage of low birthweight babies, more likely complications at childbirth, and higher health costs.

Piscotty said that attempts to bring services to low-income women must be aggressive. "You're going to need to go out to them. They're not going to come in for educational programs."

Another approach is to use incentives that encourage women to receive prenatal care. Some hospitals use coupons that are good for free items, such as a car seat, if the women obtain regular prenatal care, says Stone of Rynne Marketing Group.

The future of childbirth services will be increasingly competitive, as hospitals and health providers in most markets compete for a stable number of pregnant women. Any hospital expansion to attract these women must be financed by increased market share, because the growth of managed care will restrict rising prices.

While managed care makes cost savings essential, women's demands for the best possible birth experience will remain high. The shorter hospital stays demanded by insurers give hospitals, obstetrician-gynecologists, and midwives many opportunities to provide after-delivery care that helps with breast-feeding and other needs. The boundaries of childbirth care and competition for that care are likely to expand well beyond the hospital or physician's office.

Striving for Conception: Infertility Treatment

If maternity services are the bread and butter of hospitals, infertility services are the caviar. Over the past decade, the number of clinics offering high-tech in-vitro services has grown from 30 to 300. Infertility treatment has also become more expensive, and potentially more profitable. One of the most successful clinics, at New York Hospital-Cornell Medical Center, generates a $2 million annual surplus for the hospital and treats more than 750 patients each year.

Because insurance often does not cover infertility treatment, hospitals and physicians charge what the market will bear. Ten states required insurance companies to cover all or part of infertility treatment in 1995; the rest left it to the marketplace. With the average cost of one in-vitro procedure at $7,800, infertile couples can easily spend $20,000 or more attempting to have a baby. Experts have estimated infertility spending at $350 million annually.

Yet hospitals have discovered the hazards in offering infertility services. Mt. Sinai Hospital in New York paid $4 million in 1994 to former patients to resolve claims that the hospital overstated the success rates for its in-vitro clinic. Others, including Evanston Hospital in Chicago, have closed their in-vitro laboratories. With costly equipment and a specialized staff, clinics must have a high volume of patients to break even. In November 1995, *Forbes* predicted a future shakeout in infertility services that would include fewer programs and lower prices. In such an environment, marketing in-vitro and other infertility services will be increasingly important.

Infertility has plagued women at least since Biblical times. Contemporary researchers have found that men and women are equally likely to be infertile, and have developed an armament of drugs, surgical procedures, and laboratory procedures. The birth in 1978 of Louise Brown, a baby born from an egg fertilized in a test tube, launched a new era of hope for infertile couples.

Between 1973 and 1991, prescriptions for the ovulation-inducing

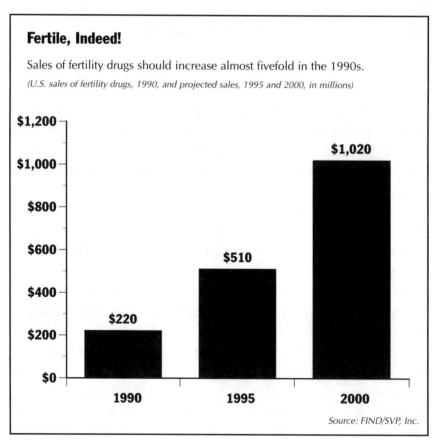

Fertile, Indeed!

Sales of fertility drugs should increase almost fivefold in the 1990s.

(U.S. sales of fertility drugs, 1990, and projected sales, 1995 and 2000, in millions)

Source: FIND/SVP, Inc.

drug clomiphene nearly doubled. Total spending on fertility drugs has increased from $220 million in 1990 to $510 million in 1995, according to FIND/SVP. Sales should hit $1 billion by 2000, with a compound annual growth rate of 17 percent between 1990 and 2000.

Most Americans want to have children. A 1990 Gallup poll found that 84 percent of childless adults under age 40 wanted children. Infertility, the inability to conceive after a year of trying to become pregnant, affects about 5.3 million American women, or 10 percent of the reproductive-age population, according to the American Society for Reproductive Medicine. Most don't go to the doctor for help, but the number who do seek help has increased. By 1987, 1.4 million Americans had gotten help for infertility, compared with 1.1 million Americans in 1981.

Treatment is a gamble. Fewer than half of Americans who seek help are successfully treated using conventional infertility treatment such as drugs or surgery. Those who decide to seek more expensive treatment, such as in-vitro fertilization and other similar methods, face far lower odds of conception. The average success rate for in-vitro fertilization is 20 percent for women under age 40. Success rates for other assisted reproduction technologies are higher, including a 30 percent success rate for women who use someone else's eggs.

The early years of marketing in-vitro infertility services included an abundance of free publicity. Throughout the 1980s, facilities such as Strong Memorial Hospital at the University of Rochester Medical Center regularly held press conferences to introduce the public to babies born using new fertilization methods. The proud mother and father, their healthy newborn baby, and their infertility doctor were celebrated by newspaper and television reporters. But by 1996, more than 40,000 babies had been conceived using in-vitro fertilization and similar methods, making stories about yet another miracle baby of limited news value. Marketers had to turn elsewhere for publicity about their programs.

In many areas, infertility marketing is a low-key affair that focuses on educational seminars. "Our practice doesn't do any paid advertising," says Kara Wiesner, office manager for the Reproductive Specialty

Center in Milwaukee. "We do more in the line of free public forums and lectures." Other centers use newspaper and radio advertisements and World Wide Web pages to sell their product. A World Wide Web page for Geisinger Medical Center even included a film of "a sperm cell in action."

Pacific Fertility Medical Center, a West coast practice with offices throughout California, offers women 90 percent of their money back if they don't become pregnant. The offer, which is advertised extensively on the radio in California and in newspaper ads as far afield as New York City, cleverly limits the risk patients undertake in a conventional in-vitro program.

"It's very appealing to patients who have had negative outcomes elsewhere," says Mary Franck, office manager for the Torrance Center of Pacific Fertility. "Even patients who haven't gone elsewhere are willing to gamble a little bit. We are telling them, if we cannot give you the take-home baby you're here to get, we'll only charge you 10 percent."

The program works by targeting women most likely to have a successful outcome from the procedure, and by charging a single price that is higher than women would pay without the guarantee. Women must be under 40 years old. Women aged 36 to 39 paid $16,500 in 1996, while women under age 36 paid $12,500. The national average for one in-vitro fertilization cycle is $7,800. Women must be willing to undergo in-vitro fertilization and fertilization with frozen embroyos if the first procedure does not work.

The program sets Pacific Fertility Centers apart from other fertility programs in the competitive California marketplace. The financial risk Pacific Fertility Centers are willing to take is a measure of what other practices may do to gain patients in the future.

Effective future marketing of infertility services will depend on:

- Appealing to a shrinking pool of women in the key ages for infertility;
- Reaching out to infertile women with educational material about their problem;

- Offering realistic estimates of success; and
- Enhancing service to patients, particularly in areas with competitive facilities.

One major source of patients for infertility clinics has been women who delayed childbearing until their late 30s. As women age, their chances of becoming pregnant get smaller. Between 1976 and 1988, the number of couples without children between 35 and 44 who experienced difficulties with infertility increased 37 percent.

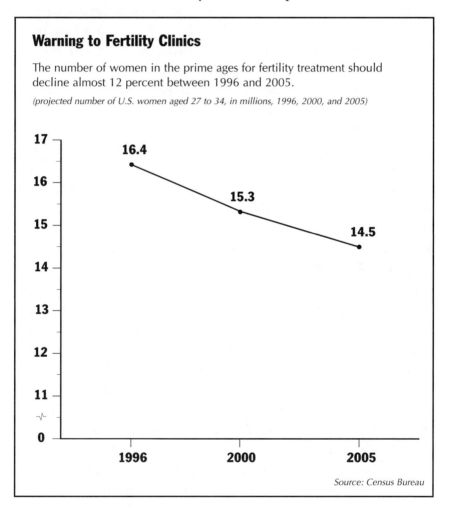

Warning to Fertility Clinics

The number of women in the prime ages for fertility treatment should decline almost 12 percent between 1996 and 2005.

(projected number of U.S. women aged 27 to 34, in millions, 1996, 2000, and 2005)

16.4

15.3

14.5

1996　　　　2000　　　　2005

Source: Census Bureau

There is no comprehensive data about the age at which patients are treated for infertility. But health providers suggest that the peak years for infertility treatment range from 27 to 34. The number of women in this age group is expected to decrease 6 percent between 1996 and 2000, from 16.4 million to 15.3 million, as the youngest baby boomers enter their late 30s. This population is expected to drop again by the year 2005, to 14.5 million. Between 1995 and 2005, the population of women most likely to seek infertility treatment will drop 11 percent, with 1.8 million fewer women.

This substantial drop in the population does not necessarily mean the demand for infertility services will be reduced. It does mean that marketers must attract a higher percentage of available couples to infertility services in order to treat the same number of patients in the future. This may indeed happen, because the market for infertility services is far from saturated. Most infertile couples still do not seek treatment for their problem.

Government scrutiny has made it essential for infertility clinics to present forthright discussions of their success rates. The company IVF America, which operates a number of U.S. clinics, signed a consent decree in 1993 after the Federal Trade Commission charged it with exaggerating its success rates. Sophisticated information is also essential to appeal to the well-educated women who have both the money and the desire for infertility assistance.

Enhanced patient service should also make a difference in competitive markets. Limiting the waiting time and receiving what they consider quality care is particularly important to the patients at Milwaukee's Reproductive Specialty Center. "Many of our patients are women in a professional field, so their time is very important," says Wiesner.

The shape of future marketing of infertility services depends on whether the service is covered by insurance. More insurance coverage would greatly increase the number of couples seeking treatment, make marketing the services easier, and could force infertility providers to offer their services at lower prices in order to have the service covered. Future technological advances may also invigorate the field, especially if they improve success rates. As the population of women in the age group seeking infertility services declines, marketers will have to work harder to sell their promise of a "take-home" baby.

Chapter 3

A Fertile Market: Products for the Childbearing Years

In 1980, Bob Perlstein saw a new market whenever he saw a pregnant woman. Here was a large group of consumers just waiting to spend money on a new baby. But there was no simple way to get in touch with the approximately 4 million Americans who are pregnant at any one time. "I thought that if I could reach women in the first trimester, what power that would be," remembers Perlstein.

To grab their attention, Perlstein offered obstetricians the chance to give away free merchandise to pregnant women. It worked very, very well. In 1996, Perlstein's company—Lifestyle Change Communications in Atlanta—is a big reason why pregnant women receive a barrage of free samples, coupons, and direct mail in the weeks after discovering they are pregnant.

New parents also spend an average of $5,000 in baby's first year of life on everything from health products to furniture. Perlstein's company, which distributes about 10 million free gift packs annually, now competes in a vigorous marketplace for products geared to women in their reproductive years.

Many of the key products for childbearing women did not exist when the baby-boom peaked in the late 1950s. The staggering success of birth-control pills, home pregnancy tests, and new feminine-hygiene products such as "mini-pads" has positioned women in their childbearing years as the primary consumers for many drugs and other products. Home pregnancy tests had sales of $191 million in 1994-95, according to ACNielsen, and sanitary napkins and tampons had sales of $1.7 billion during the same period.

Products for the childbearing years must be sold with caution, however. Product failures such as the Rely tampon, which was pulled in 1980 after it was proven to cause toxic shock syndrome, are a warning that this market requires the highest standards of safety, security, and trust. Women of childbearing age have a strong desire for new inventions and technology, but they will not touch any product if it has a remote chance of endangering their health.

Twelve Times a Year

They aren't just absorbent pads. Today they have "wings" and "curves" and "ultra thin" profiles. Yet the basic message in marketing sanitary napkins and tampons, freedom and dependability, has remained the same for decades.

When sanitary napkins were first marketed in 1921, they truly offered a new type of freedom for women. Until that time, women made their own sanitary protection at home, typically out of material which was then laundered and reused.

A 1927 advertisement for Kotex, the first disposable sanitary napkin, promised "The Safe Solution of Women's Greatest Hygienic Problem." Using Kotex, women could "go about for hours" and "meet all situations without a second thought." Later that year, advertisers promised that the product was used by "8 in 10 better class women."

Tampons were first marketed in the U.S. in 1936 by Dr. Earle C. Haas, a Denver physician first trained as a barber. He attributed his inspiration to the plug-shaped bandage used in military hospitals, according to Packaged Facts. Haas was not the first person to think of tampons, however. African tribeswomen had used devices similar to tampons for years before Haas's discovery.

Tampons and sanitary napkins quickly became fixtures in American households. Feminine-hygiene products today are purchased by 82 percent of American women aged 12 to 49, according to Packaged Facts.

Yet the relationship between the American woman and her menstrual products has been marred by problems. For years, manufacturers have struggled with the problem of tampons that leak. Even today, as many as 40 percent of women use tampons and pads at the same time to deal with the problem, according to Packaged Facts.

The Toxic Shock Legacy

In the late 1970s, tampon manufacturers believed they had solved the problem with new tampons that contained superabsorbent fibers called polyacrylates. The tampons were marketed aggressively and quickly gained in popularity. Then tragedy struck, as hundreds and then thousands of American women developed a previously rare disease called toxic shock syndrome. By the fall of 1980, the Centers for Disease Control reported that 70 percent of women with the disease had been using Procter & Gamble's polyacrylate product, the Rely tampon. After pressure from the Food and Drug Administration, the company pulled the tampon off the market that same year.

Toxic shock syndrome was most disastrous to the 88 women who died of toxic shock syndrome and the 2,000 women who had developed the disease by 1983. But it was also costly to Procter & Gamble and to the tampon industry in general. Procter & Gamble announced to employees that the cost of stopping production and distribution of Rely was $75 million. The company and its insurers paid even more out of court and in confidential settlements linked to the product, according to Alicia Swasy, author of a book on Procter & Gamble called *Soap Opera*.

Tampon sales plummeted in the middle 1980s, in part due to the government's finding that the use of any tampon increases the risk of toxic shock syndrome for menstruating women. However, sales of tampons have risen since then. The elimination of highly absorbent tampons such as Rely and the distribution of knowledge about toxic shock syndrome have greatly reduced the incidence of the disease. Tampons now are required to include information about toxic shock syndrome. But tampons still make up only 40 percent of retail sales in the menstrual-products market, according to ACNielsen.

The legacy of the toxic shock crisis is more caution among women using tampons. One sign of this is the difficulty that generic and private-label tampons have had in gaining a niche in the market. Private-label or "store brand" tampons had about 4 percent of the market in 1995, while private-label sanitary napkins and pads had about 14 percent, according to *Private Label*, a magazine that tracks store-branded products. Women are more hesitant to try a new brand that is used inside the body than they are to try a new brand for external protection, according to *Private Label*.

Tampax cleverly draws on the sense of risk women feel in using an internal protection product with its slogan, "Trust is Tampax." But this product is doubly complicated by the fact that girls begin using tampons and sanitary napkins in adolescence, a life stage notorious for embarrassment, insecurity, and awkwardness. Marketers must know how to talk to adolescents as well as women in order to sell their product. The teenage market is particularly important because women generally don't switch products once they find one they like, says Robert LePre of the New England Consulting Group in Westport, Connecticut. "Once you're in your mid teens or older teens, that's it," says LePre, the former U.S. general manager for Tambrands, manufacturer of Tampax.

Selling the Message

Educational efforts are a central marketing strategy of Tampax, says Janey Loyd of Tambrands. Tambrands focuses on building brand loyalty early, with education programs for 6th and 9th grade girls. The company sends materials and sometimes even lecturers to schools. Another educational effort is the Tampax home page on the World Wide Web, which includes information on the female reproductive system and a do-it-yourself chart about how to predict a woman's period.

The company's experience with the educational program is a reminder that while the sexual revolution has come and gone, young girls are still overwhelmed by the predictable passage of adolescence. "It's less of a commercial Tampax sell than helping girls understand the changes that are occurring," says Loyd. "We talk to coaches who have promising athletes that drop out of sports when they start menstruating. You say, 'Things must have changed,' but things haven't changed."

Procter & Gamble has not introduced another tampon since the Rely disaster. But the company spent up to $100 million on advertising for its new sanitary napkin Always in 1984, according to Packaged Facts. By 1989, Always was the market leader, and it has remained one of the top-two sellers ever since.

The perennial themes of freedom and security continue to be promoted in advertisements, but the industry has also latched on to many new appeals to contemporary women. Johnson & Johnson promotes its OB tampon as a woman-created product that is a clear alternative to the market leader, Tampax. "The tampon you probably use was designed half a century ago, by a man," says the athletic narrator in a 1993 television ad. "A woman—a gynecologist—designed OB." Tampax promotes its biodegradable product and recycled box, and Johnson & Johnson focuses on working women in commercials such as a 1992 appeal for Stayfree pads. "Oh, what a disaster," a well-dressed woman says. "Instead of running to the meeting, I ran to the ladies room." Then a voiceover announces, "Whose monthly protection hasn't failed?"

Future Sales

The population of American women aged 12 to 49 will remain roughly the same over the next two decades, so marketers of menstrual protection products in the U.S. will gain revenue mainly by taking it away from their competitors. Increased prices are already more likely than increased sales to account for profits, according to Packaged Facts. Price increases are one reason why retail dollar volume of the menstrual products market is expected to climb over $2 billion by 1998.

To be successful in the future, menstrual marketers must:

- Market and educate teenagers;
- Offer products to older women;
- Focus on price; and
- Cultivate working women.

Some market changes should help to counteract the stable number of menstruating women. One positive trend for marketers is a long-term decrease in the average age when girls begin menstruating. The reason for the drop is unclear. The average age of menstruation today is about 12, compared with 13 in the 1950s and 14 in 1900, according to About Women Inc. and Packaged Facts.

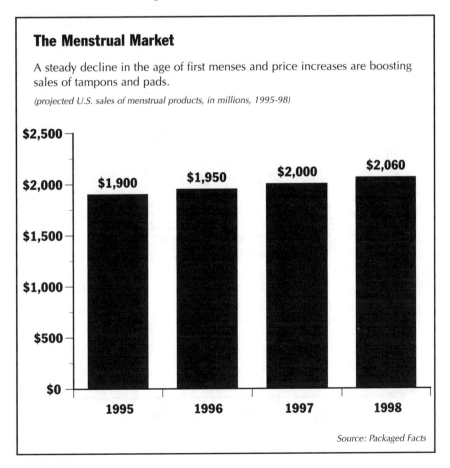

The Menstrual Market

A steady decline in the age of first menses and price increases are boosting sales of tampons and pads.

(projected U.S. sales of menstrual products, in millions, 1995-98)

Source: Packaged Facts

Educational marketing to girls must start early. "I think the companies have to double or triple their efforts at educating young girls about menstruation and how to deal with it," says LePre. In many parts of the country, there is still no school education about menstruation because school officials do not want any education linked to sex. Marketers who find a way to reach young girls are most likely to attract them as customers over the next 30 years.

Older women are another group that could boost sales of hygiene products. Women past their childbearing years already buy some menstrual products. Many women use them during hormone replacement therapy because of sporadic bleeding. In 1995, 14.5 percent of 55-to-64

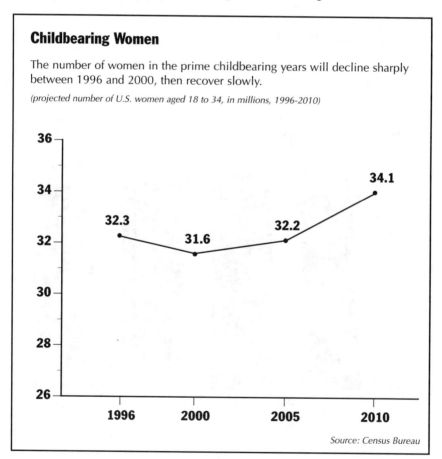

Childbearing Women

The number of women in the prime childbearing years will decline sharply between 1996 and 2000, then recover slowly.

(projected number of U.S. women aged 18 to 34, in millions, 1996-2010)

Source: Census Bureau

year old American women used sanitary napkins and 4 percent used tampons, according to Simmons Market Research Bureau. Older women also use sanitary products if they have slight incontinence problems.

Manufacturers have just started marketing directly to older women. A 1995 advertisement for the Carefree Ultra Dry Pantiliner suggests that the product is perfect for protection during "light period flow, and even from light urine wetness." The growth in the mid-life and elderly markets in the future should make these messages more common.

Marketers of brand-name products also must be ready to match the lower prices of generic and private-label products, which may pose a long-term threat. Sales of private-label tampons increased 20 percent in 1995, a far greater increase than the overall 1 percent growth in tampon sales, according to *Private Label.*

The popularity of private-label products stems in part from the increasing tendency of American women to buy their sanitary protection at mass-merchandise stores such as WalMart. The percentage of sanitary napkins sold at mass outlets increased 12 percent from 1994 to 1995, while the percentage of sanitary napkins sold in supermarkets declined 2 percent, according to ACNielsen.

Working women dominate all adult segments of the menstrual market, and they place a premium on feminine-hygiene products that are convenient, easy to carry, and discrete. Demand for this type of product is reflected in a number of sanitary napkins, such as Always Quickwraps, that come with their own wrapper so they can be carried and disposed of easily. Working women should be particularly receptive to technological advances that produce better tampons.

The continuing taboos surrounding conversation about menstrual periods are a barrier, but they also offer rich educational opportunities for product marketers. Marketers of other products in the feminine-hygiene category, such as yeast-infection products and douches, face similar problems in educating consumers about their products.

From "News" to Spring Flowers

Yeast-infection medication and douches are most popular among black, southern women, according to Simmons Market Research Bureau. But the innovative marketing strategies of these products could serve as a model of judicious target marketing, and of the different approaches to the stark truth of feminine-hygiene products.

When over-the-counter treatments for yeast infections were approved in 1991, manufacturers began campaigns to persuade women that they could purchase yeast-infection medication over the counter more easily than they could through their physician. Johnson & Johnson's Monistat 7 cost the company $42 million to launch, according to Packaged Facts.

Women responded eagerly to the products, suggesting there was a huge unmet need. By 1992, sales of over-the-counter yeast-infection products were higher than prescription sales had been before the products were sold directly to consumers. In 1994, sales of yeast-infection products were an estimated $595 million, according to Packaged Facts.

The products were marketed on television and in magazines, using dramatically different techniques. A 1993 television advertisement for Monistat 7 makes the product sound more like a pair of bedroom slippers than medicine. A woman compares Monistat with another product that is "dry, hard," and concludes: "Soft, gentle Monistat, fits natural, feels natural."

But some print advertisements for the products were starkly honest. A 1993 magazine advertisement targeted information-loving women with lots of text in newsletter form. The text mentioned "itching, burning and discharge," with copious information about the problem. Information-rich advertising is a good fit, because consumers of yeast-infection medication are more likely than average to have attended college, according to Simmons.

A 1995-96 advertising battle between Monistat 7 and Diflucan, a prescription yeast-infection treatment in pill form, hinged on the use of technical information that was not even shared with most consumers a decade ago. Advertisements in a 1995 women's magazine for Diflucan show a radiant female pilot standing in front of an airplane. The advertisements boast about the fact that Diflucan treats yeast infections with one tablet taken once, which is perfect for this obviously busy professional. The most unusual part of the advertisement is its stark admission that 13 percent of women who take the drug develop headaches and 7 percent feel nauseated. Is the convenience of Diflucan worth the risk? Unlike most health advertisements, the text reveals the trade-off women should be aware of from the start.

A 1996 advertisement for Monistat 7, which must be taken for seven days, suggests that convenience should be the least of women's con-

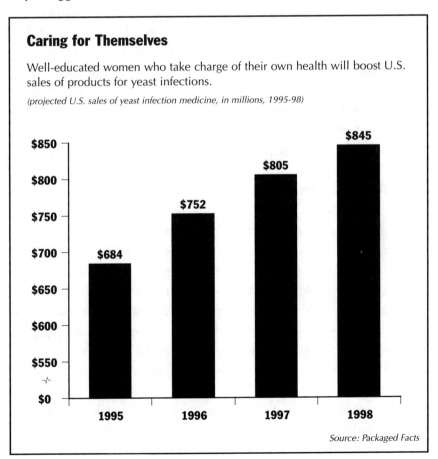

Caring for Themselves

Well-educated women who take charge of their own health will boost U.S. sales of products for yeast infections.

(projected U.S. sales of yeast infection medicine, in millions, 1995-98)

Source: Packaged Facts

cerns. The advertisement warns that 26 percent of women taking flu-
conazole, the drug contained in Diflucan, develop side effects. It also
mentions that other drugs' interaction with Diflucan could create
unknown effects.

The combative focus of the Monistat 7 advertisement may become
more common in this category as the size of the customer base shrinks.
Women aged 18 to 34 are most likely to use yeast-infection products.
This group is predicted to be 2 percent smaller in 2000 than it was in
1996, and less than 1 percent smaller in 2005 than it was in 1996. This
group will not grow beyond 1995 levels until about 2006.

Future sales of yeast-infection products are expected to slow down
to about 5 percent annual growth in sales because of the drop in the
number of women in the age group, according to Packaged Facts. The
company predicts that more companies will enter the market with
low-priced brands. Sales are projected to reach $845 million by 1998,
due in part to the proven safety of the products. Up to 13 million
American women develop at least one yeast-infection a year. Seventy-
five percent of all American women will develop at least one yeast-
infection in their lifetime.

Springtime and Flowers

The users of vaginal douching and cleansing products are an entirely
different market. The products are used extensively: 48 percent of
American women used them in 1995, according to Simmons Market
Research Bureau. Total sales were about $200 million in 1993, according
to Packaged Facts. But their marketing uses the indirect approach, with
no mention of sexual intercourse. Instead, the products are typically
marketed using images of beautiful women and flowers.

A 1991 television advertisement for Summer's Eve Feminine Wash has
a woman singing the words: "I was dreaming of summer, cool breeze,
and fresh air. When I want that feeling, Summer's Eve takes me there."

The roundabout way of selling these products fits their profile customer and the lack of medical support for the products. The typical

douche customer has a household income of less than $30,000 annually, and she is likely to be a high school drop-out.

Marketers cannot use health experts to sell douche products, so harder-edge advertisements are difficult to imagine. Studies have found that douches contribute to yeast infections, and many physicians advise patients against using them. For these reasons, the growth of this market should be slow.

The differences in marketing these two products reflects the differences in their markets. Though women as a group are becoming more demanding about health-care information and products, the marketing of douches shows how some products of dubious health value can still be sold to a less-educated audience. Women who like douches are loyal customers, and their desire for a fresh feeling outweighs their concern about other health problems.

"Calendar Fear" and Contraceptives

Controversy has followed contraceptives since well before birth-control pills were developed. For years, they could not be marketed to customers. Until the 1930s, it was illegal to write about contraceptives in U. S. magazines or even medical journals.

The taboo nature of this topic forced early marketing efforts to become masterpieces of allusion and omission. In the 1920s, Lysol disinfectant commonly marketed itself as a contraceptive, though advertisers dared not use the phrase "birth control," according to advertising historian Roland Marchand. A 1927 magazine advertisement features a meticulously dressed mother sitting on a stool as her voluptuous daughter slouches in a flouncy dress on a nearby chair. "Read this book carefully, dear...It explains things so much better than I can," the advertisement promises. To readers of the day, the ad's reference to "intimate problems" and "peace of mind" would have been clearly understood as referring to birth control. Another Lysol ad in 1932 publicized "calendar fear," which occurs due to a "feminine irregularity." Lysol's promise to "kill germs" was meant to be read as "kill sperm," according to Marchand.

The subject was not defused by the sexual revolution. In the 1960s, critics blamed promoters of oral contraceptives for everything from launching the sexual revolution to failing to warn women of health risks. The pill was not advertised directly to consumers in the 1960s, but its dramatic advantages were eagerly described in women's magazines and other periodicals. "Modern woman is at last free, as a man is free, to dispose of her own body, to earn a living...to try a successful career," wrote an ecstatic Claire Booth Luce. The discovery of health risks connected to the pill, including an increased risk of stroke, lead to the 1969 publication of *The Doctors' Case Against the Pill.* Widespread publicity about these health hazards dampened women's enthusiasm for the product somewhat, and led to the strategy of cautious use that continues to the present.

The pill actually fared much better than did other recent contraceptives. In the 1970s, A.H. Robins was widely criticized for its marketing of the Dalkon Shield intrauterine device as safe and effective after it was linked to patient deaths and serious injury. The company ultimately paid more than $40 million in legal settlements after the device was pulled from the market. The marketing of contraception in the 1990s is heavily limited by the media, and marketers are still criticized for promoting sex and overpromoting unsafe methods. The high level of scrutiny in this area means that contraceptive manufacturers must have a strong stomach for controversy, good legal counsel, a high sensitivity to potential marketing minefields, and a good product.

Many critics suggest that the market for contraceptives is stalled because there are so many obstacles to profit. "Ten or 15 years ago, you had 15 or so companies producing the pill. Now it's 3," says Susan LaMontagne, vice president for media relations for Planned Parenthood Federation.

Yet women continue to demand contraceptives and the market is expected to grow rapidly, in spite of the stable population in this age group. The U. S. market for contraceptive drugs is expected to increase to $2.7 billion by the year 2000, an 80 percent increase over the $1.7 billion market in 1996, according to FIND/SVP. This includes the pill, the most frequently used contraceptive. About 29 percent of women using contraceptives used the pill in 1990. Over-the-counter contraceptives, including foams, female condoms, and male condoms, added up to $287 million in 1994-95, according to ACNielsen.

Since those early days of calendar fear, contraceptives have become a central part of American life. About 59 percent of American women used either reversible contraceptives or sterilization in 1990. Most

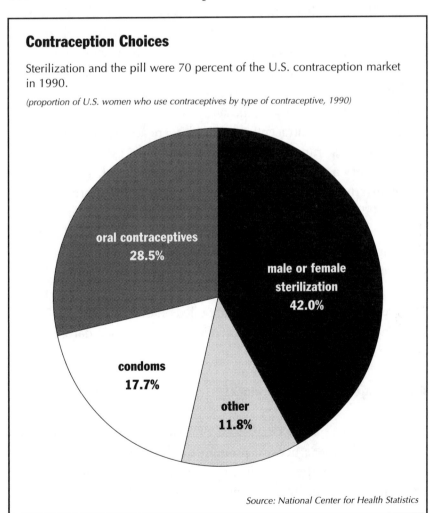

Contraception Choices

Sterilization and the pill were 70 percent of the U.S. contraception market in 1990.

(proportion of U.S. women who use contraceptives by type of contraceptive, 1990)

oral contraceptives
28.5%

male or female
sterilization
42.0%

condoms
17.7%

other
11.8%

Source: National Center for Health Statistics

women use reversible contraception, but 42 percent used sterilization of themselves or a partner.

Womens' birth-control choices are influenced by their age, their income, and their racial or ethnic identity. Younger women are more likely than older women to use reversible contraceptives because they want the option of becoming pregnant later. Among the 32 percent of 15-to-19-year-olds who use contraceptives, 52 percent use the pill and 44 percent use condoms.

The pill is most likely to be used by women under age 25. Women aged 30 to 44 are more likely than younger women, to be sterilized and black and Hispanic women are more likely than white women to choose female sterilization. The diaphragm is used by fewer than 3 percent of women, but it is used most often by women who are over age 30, white, married, and college-educated.

A series of new contraceptive methods were added to the market in the 1990s. These range from Depo-Provera, a hormone that must be injected every month, to Norplant, another hormone that must be surgically inserted and removed. A female condom was approved by the FDA in 1993. The manufacturers of Depo-Provera, largely considered the most successful of the three, claimed in their 1996 ads that more than 1 million women use the contraceptive, which is more than use the diaphragm.

These new methods supersede other methods that continue to fail. Most recently, the Today sponge was pulled off the market in 1995 when manufacturers said it couldn't meet new government standards for safety at the factory.

AIDS Invigorates Condom Market

The use of condoms has expanded dramatically since the emergence of AIDS in the 1980s, because properly used condoms can usually prevent the spread of the HIV virus that causes AIDS and other sexually transmitted diseases. In fact, condoms were first developed by ancient

Egyptians to protect the penis against a parasite spread through water, according to scholars Joseph G. Schenker and Vicki Rabenou.

Young women are increasingly more likely to purchase condoms. The majority (55 percent) of women having intercourse for the first time in 1988-1990 used a condom, compared with about 28 percent in 1980-1982. Such trends have encouraged condom manufacturers to advertise directly to women.

Ancel, which makes "Lifestyle" condoms, launched an ambitious ad campaign directed to women in 1995. The campaign featured a woman wearing a false big nose and glasses with the caption, "You wouldn't believe what I used to go through to buy condoms." The ad, which ran in major women's magazines, offered information about the brand's color-coding system that makes it easier to buy the products quickly at the store. The Ancel ads also offered an 800 number to call for a free sample, a dollar-off coupon, free literature about the product, and the chance to enter a sweepstakes with grand-prize trips to Cancun or Colorado. In return, the company gained the names and addresses of women interested in information about condoms. Postal service regulations prohibit sending contraceptives in the mail unless a consumer asks for them.

Ancel's overall message could have been taken directly from *Our Bodies, Our Selves*. Women "don't have to be embarrassed" about buying condoms, says Kimberly Hughes, marketing assistant for Ancel in Eatontown, New Jersey. "They should take their own health into consideration."

Another product with a similar marketing message is the female condom, Reality, whose 1995 ad campaign had the message: "Count on Yourself." But the tumultuous launching of the female condom offers yet another example of the numerous marketing challenges in the contraceptive market. After a start that many contraceptive experts labeled slow, the Female Health Company, the company that produces the condom, said sales were rising steadily in mid-1996.

When it was first introduced, the product received immense publicity as the first female birth-control device to protect against pregnancy and sexually transmitted diseases. Once the product was available in the market, the media were no longer interested. "They said, 'Oh, we did that story already,'" says Holly Sherman, spokesman for the Female Health Company of Chicago and London. Stories that did appear were often negative, such as a 1994 story in *Working Woman* that criticized the product for being "so new and hard to find that few women have tried them." The article also criticized the product for squeaking if used improperly.

The company realized it had to respond to the perceptions that its product was hard to use, cumbersome, and costly. The unusual appearance of the product did not help. "It looks more complicated to use than it actually is," says Sherman. Current efforts include an expanded advertising campaign in a wide range of magazines and an expensive offer of free samples to women who want to try the product. In March 1996, the company was receiving thousands of calls every week for free samples, an effort Sherman considered essential so women could realize that the product is not difficult to use. "People ask me about the disadvantages," says Sherman. "Anything in the world of contraceptives is controversial."

Preventing Pregnancy

Another challenge for the female condom is the fact that most women choose contraception to prevent pregnancy, not to prevent disease. Most contraceptive marketing reflects this concern.

Upjohn's 1996 advertisements for Depo-Provera promoted the 99 percent effectiveness of the product and its convenience. The ads are tailored to different audiences, depending on the market. A 1996 ad for *Ebony* shows three highly fashionable black women in their 20s looking sternly off the page. "No way do I want to get pregnant," the ad reads. Another 1996 ad for *Parents* shows a young mother overseeing a trio of messy kids in a messy living room with the caption: "Things are crazy enough around here. I don't need the hassle of daily birth control."

The Depo-Provera ads also reflect the complicated nature of the contraceptive market, a market in which every product has limitations. The ads are forthright about the side effects of the drug, including irregular menstrual bleeding and weight gain.

Other products market to concerns about such problems. A 1995 magazine ad for Conceptrol, a nonprescription contraceptive gel, emphasizes that it is easy, effective, and safe—with "no hormones, nothing to alter your body's natural balance." The advertisement says nothing about the Conceptrol success rate, perhaps because contraceptive gels have a lower success rate than do most prescription products. Contraceptive gels and other over-the-counter products for women have a market share of less than 2 percent, according to Planned Parenthood.

Although most contraceptive products for women are distributed by prescription, women usually choose what they want, says Ellen Schoenberger, product manager for Depo-Provera. "The contraceptive market is consumer driven. Physicians are very likely to give patients the product they ask for. Their thoughts are, the person will be most successful with the option they want to use."

Contraceptives also are heavily marketed in college and university settings, which typically have programs about contraception and counselors for sexually active students. But contraceptive advertising continues to be largely banned on network television, and magazines for teenagers usually do not accept contraceptive advertising. "A lot of the programs that are on television are far more sexual than anything that would be in an advertisement," says Dr. Allan Rosenfield, dean of the Columbia School of Public Health. "I'm not sure why the media are so afraid of something that's less controversial than programming that goes on all the time."

One result of such limited marketing opportunities is that many women do not receive enough information about birth control. Most Americans do not talk about birth control with their physicians: 61 percent of 2,002 adults surveyed in 1995 said they had never discussed birth control with a doctor or other health professional, and only 32 percent of those surveyed had physicians who had raised the topic.

Surveys also have shown that American women are generally not satisfied with their birth control. A 1991 to 1993 study of 257 women at a Tennessee family-planning clinic found that 43 percent of women using the pill were not satisfied because of side effects, and 47 percent of women using condoms were not satisfied because they are inconvenient and uncomfortable. The survey also found that the average woman had tried more than two types of birth control on average.

Such surveys suggest the potential power of effective contraceptive marketing and the immense need for education about birth control among American women. Marketers who make education part of their mission will find an audience eager for information.

Boosting Future Sales

The aging of America's population will bring good news and bad news to contraceptive manufacturers. While the overall population of women who use contraceptives is projected to shrink, the number of teenagers who use contraceptives is projected to grow. This group is most likely to use the pill and condoms. Women aged 20 to 24 are also more likely than average to use the pill and condoms, and they are expected to decrease only slightly between 1996 and 2000. Then this group will begin a steady increase as baby boomer's children graduate from college.

The age group that will experience the biggest population drop is women aged 30 to 34. These women are less likely than younger women to use condoms or the pill, and are more likely to be sterilized. The population decline in this group should be more significant to physicians who perform sterilizations than to contraceptive manufacturers.

Predictions of big annual increases in sales of contraceptive drugs reflect the continuing strong supply of younger women and teenagers. birth-control pills should increase their U.S. sales from $1.3 billion in 1996 to over $2 billion in 2000, according to FIND/SVP. But the firm suggests that growth in alternative contraceptive sales will be even more dramatic than growth of the pill. A contraceptive patch manufactured

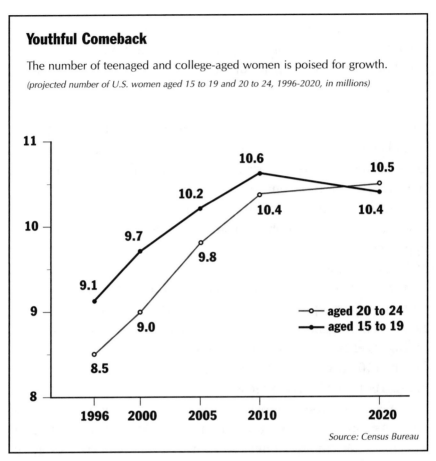

Youthful Comeback

The number of teenaged and college-aged women is poised for growth.

(projected number of U.S. women aged 15 to 19 and 20 to 24, 1996-2020, in millions)

10.6

10.5

10.2

10.4

10.4

9.7

9.8

9.1

aged 20 to 24
aged 15 to 19

9.0

8.5

1996   2000   2005   2010   2020

Source: Census Bureau

by Wyeth-Ayerst is currently in clinical trials. Products such as Depo-Provera are expected to increase their sales 16 percent a year until the year 2000, with U.S. sales of $637 million by the year 2000, says FIND/SVP.

How to Boost Sales

Contraceptive marketers must contend with many restrictions on how and where their products can be promoted. While Americans are unlikely to suddenly embrace contraceptive marketing, there are signs of change and opportunities for growth. To be successful, contraceptive marketers must:

- Offer convenience;
- Deal openly with health and pregnancy protection;
- Push the limits on where contraceptives can be advertised; and
- Segment the market.

Convenience may be the most important of these rules. The popularity of Upjohn's Depo-Provera, which is injected four times a year, suggests that the public is interested in new methods that don't require a lot of work. "We promote our product's attributes compared to the pill," says Schoenberger of Upjohn. "It's a more convenient product for women...We're always looking for an easier way out, as Americans." The appeal of contraceptives that make life easier should remain strong as long as women remain in the workplace.

Contraceptives currently on the market are an either/or proposition, with oral contraceptives providing excellent pregnancy protection but no protection against sexually transmitted diseases, and condoms providing excellent protection against sexually transmitted diseases but less than 100 percent protection against pregnancy. New products that address both concerns are needed.

One way to market a more inclusive product could be marketing women's contraceptives with condoms, says Dr. Robert A. Hatcher, director of the family planning program at Grady Memorial Hospital in Atlanta and professor of obstetrics and gynecology at Emory University. Such a method was tried years ago when a foam contraceptive was marketed in a package with condoms.

The limitations of existing contraceptives must be clearly stated in any marketing effort. This includes informing women about possible side effects and anticipating potential problems. As health consumers, women may be most vigilant in areas related to reproduction. While advertisements that clearly state side effects could discourage some women, the risk of not informing women clearly is starkly apparent.

Norplant is the latest contraceptive to be caught in a barrage of criticism. Hundreds of lawsuits have been filed against the drug's manufacturer, claiming everything from scarring and emotional distress to autoimmune problems. Attorney Roger Brosnahan was quoted in *Newsweek* in late 1995 saying, "The warnings were abominable and the overpromotion was fraudulent."

The jury is still out on whether or not Norplant is safe. Wyeth-Ayerst, manufacturer of the product, refused to discuss its marketing. But the lessons from Norplant's difficulties are important lessons for health-care marketers, who must also sell their product to women with increasingly high expectations.

The FDA requires pharmaceutical companies to publish technical information about side effects in advertisements. Drug manufacturers typically provide this information in small print. Manufacturers in the future would be well advised to explain side effects in plain English, using large print. As women learn more about health care and become better established in the work world, they will want increasingly clear information about risks and benefits. "All we hear about is convenience and availability," says Cindy Pearson, executive director of the Women's Health Network. "Almost no contraceptives are being marketed in ways that are useful to women."

With the overall number of women aged 15 to 44 expected to remain stable, contraceptive marketers must target their message to growing numbers of black, Hispanic, and Asian women. Controversies have also linked minority women and contraceptives, such as the findings in the 1960s and 1970s that the rates of female sterilization among minorities were far higher than the rates among white women. As a result, many minority women are wary of efforts to provide contraception that could be coercive.

The market for contraceptives among black and Hispanic women is large and growing steadily, even as the number of young non-Hispanic white women declines. Some time between the year 2010 and 2020, a majority of American babies will be born to minority mothers.

Social marketers use research and other techniques to "sell" everything from AIDS prevention to the use of contraception in overpopulated areas. Their experiences hold many clues for those who want to market health care to minorities and low-income groups. For example, marketers working to promote condom use among prostitutes in Tijuana, Mexico, found that the women were not worried about dying from AIDS. Rather, they were concerned about leaving their children without a parent, says Michael Ramah, a social marketer with Porter/Novelli in Washington, D.C. The group developed comic books in Spanish with sample condoms around the message, "I want to protect my child."

Marketers also should continue working to see increased acceptance of contraceptive advertising. The partial lifting of the ban against condom advertising on television in 1993 opened the door to future changes in advertising policy. Contraceptive ads on networks geared to young people, such as MTV, could be a perfect fit. As women continue to gain power as attorneys, television executives, and government officials, the archaic ban on contraceptive advertising is less likely to remain, because contraceptives are central to so many women's lives.

Domestic Science: Pregnancy and Ovulation Tests

Home pregnancy tests are usually marketed to women who want babies. Yet about half of women who buy home pregnancy tests don't want to be pregnant, according to Packaged Facts. In the early 1990s, Quidel Corporation began addressing both sides of the market. The company began selling two different home pregnancy tests: one for women who would like their test to be positive and another for women who don't want to be pregnant. One product, called Conceive, features a baby on the package. The other, called RapidVue, has no baby on the package.

The San Diego company is attempting to profit from a market that is saturated with effective products and has a slow-growing customer base. "A lot of these products are comparable," says Denise Weiser, marketing manager for Quidel. "But the other factor is emotion. You're playing on the emotions of the sale."

Thirty years ago, a pregnancy test required a trip to the doctor. The emergence of home pregnancy tests in the 1970s transformed the discovery of pregnancy from a medical experience to be shared with one's doctor to a private experience that could be shared or experienced alone. Sales of home pregnancy tests in 1994 were about $232 million, according to Packaged Facts.

Home pregnancy tests take from 1 to 15 minutes to offer results. Their use soared during the 1980s, and about 41 percent of U.S. women who think they're pregnant now use them, according to Packaged Facts.

But a diminishing supply of women aged 18 to 34 means that the market for home pregnancy tests will be more competitive in the future. The number of the youngest pregnancy-test users is expected to grow, with steady growth in women aged 15 to 19. Women aged 18 to 24 are the group most likely to use home pregnancy tests, according to Simmons Market Research Bureau. Nearly 6 out of 10 women buyers get their home pregnancy tests at drugstores, with the remaining purchases split roughly equally between supermarkets and mass market stores, according to ACNielsen.

Current marketing strategies use advertisements on television, in women's magazines, and the World Wide Web. A Warner-Lambert "Women's Care" page offers information about its e.p.t. test and two toll-free "helplines" staffed with nurses—one for Spanish speakers and one for English speakers.

Advertisements generally focus on accuracy, ease of use, and the world of marital baby-lust. An advertisement for Carter-Wallace's First Response shows a man and a woman embracing, with the caption: "It's the most important test of your life. Why take a chance?" A television commercial for Warner-Lambert's e.p.t. showed a real couple just after a test, with the woman crying as her husband says, "We'll keep trying." When the woman in the commercial eventually got pregnant, the product gained free publicity.

More than one-third (37 percent) of home pregnancy test users are single, divorced, separated, or widowed, according to Simmons Market Research Bureau. Single women are more likely than married women to use the test. Such women are increasingly likely to want babies of their own: the number of births to unmarried women nearly tripled between 1970 and 1992, and 30 percent of new mothers in 1992 were unmarried.

Marketers of home pregnancy tests could target teenagers and single women as potential growth markets. Some may emulate Quidel's strategy of plain-package marketing. Quidel even charges less for its RapidVue "Babyless" product than it does for Conceive. "It's like what Charles Revson said about cosmetics: People buy hope," says Quidel chief executive Steven Franklin in *Forbes*. "In our case, they pay more for hope than for possible relief."

Single women and teens hoping they are not pregnant are most likely to want simple tests that work well and are reasonably priced. A key challenge for marketers in the future will be to maintain their core

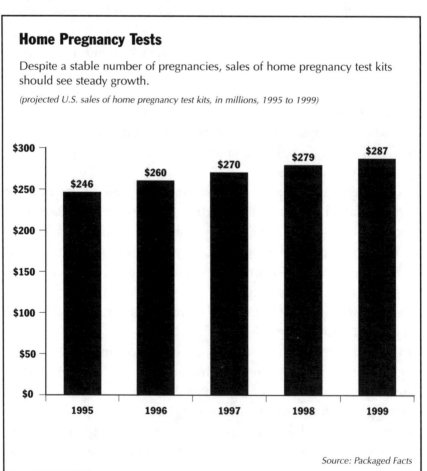

Home Pregnancy Tests

Despite a stable number of pregnancies, sales of home pregnancy test kits should see steady growth.

(projected U.S. sales of home pregnancy test kits, in millions, 1995 to 1999)

1995	$246
1996	$260
1997	$270
1998	$279
1999	$287

Source: Packaged Facts

group of customers while attracting the increasing number of teens and single women who want to take that "most important test" at home.

Predicting the Future

The photo is a tear-jerker, with a tiny baby hand holding on to its mother's finger for dear life. "One step closer to pregnancy," the copy reads. For women who want to become pregnant, this advertisement for Clearplan Easy—an ovulation detector—is a commercial roadmap to pregnancy.

Ovulation detectors tell a woman when she is most fertile and likely to conceive. They are a new and flourishing product category, thanks to

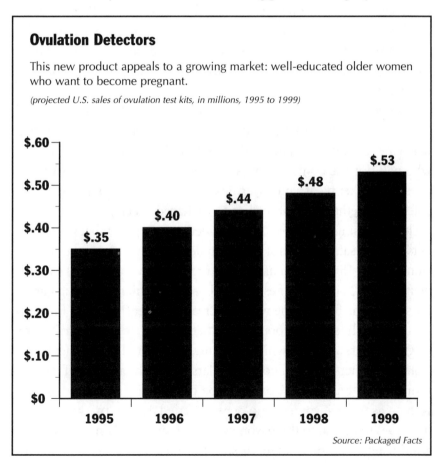

Ovulation Detectors

This new product appeals to a growing market: well-educated older women who want to become pregnant.

(projected U.S. sales of ovulation test kits, in millions, 1995 to 1999)

Source: Packaged Facts

a large number of baby-boom women who are trying to have children in their 30s and 40s. Sales of ovulation detectors were an estimated $35 million in 1995, 21 percent more than in 1994, according to Packaged Facts. Product sales are expected to reach $53 million in 1999.

The products are most commonly used by women aged 25 to 34, according to Simmons. This group is expected to decline by 7 percent between 1996 and 2000, then drop another 2 percent by the year 2005. Yet the market for ovulation detectors is far from saturated, with fewer than 2 percent of American women using the kits annually, according to Simmons. Ovulation kits are unlike pregnancy tests because they require prior knowledge about how the body works and why such a kit could help a woman conceive. The kits detect a hormone that is present just before ovulation. Their market is well-educated, careful planners who have relatively well-ordered lives. But the ultimate market for ovulation kits is about one in ten couples, because that is the portion who struggle with infertility.

Technological changes may also boost the size of this market. Quidel is testing a product that uses hormone measurement to tell women when they are infertile. The product, SafePlan, could be used by women who will not use contraceptives. Another technological boost is the possible marketing of a men's fertility test. This product is already available in the Netherlands, according to Packaged Facts.

The increasing success of ovulation detectors is proof that new products that are safe and useful will be in demand, even as the number of women aged 15 to 44 remains stable (or declines very slightly) over the next decade. Marketers of established products will need to dig harder for sales in the future. One way to increase market share is to focus on parts of the childbearing population that continue to grow, particularly single mothers and non-white, Hispanic, Asian, or black mothers.

Single mothers spend billions of dollars on health care, even if they are more likely than other women to be poor. This includes divorced women as well as women who never married. Health marketers must find ways to appeal to these women, whose image of family may mean good friends, other women, or simply children. Advertisements for contraceptives, ovulation detectors and other health products must show women and children without husbands, not simply images of conventionally married women with children. Because single mothers are less affluent than other mothers, low prices and good value are of particular importance to them.

Marketers of health services, such as birth centers and physicians, must strive to make women without husbands feel comfortable alone or with a partner who is not a husband. This may include offering special programs for childbirth to single women, or providing child care or child play areas while women receive their own health care.

Marketing to the increasing share of Hispanic, Asian, and black mothers also should pay off, as birth rates in these groups continues to climb. Spanish-language marketing of products, health information, and services provides information to women who are far more likely to be pregnant than is the average American woman. Sponsorships of ethnic music festivals, scholarship funds, or other activities or causes important to minority women also send a message to these women that their needs are important.

On a more practical level, companies must offer a Spanish-speaking option on help lines for childbirth-related products. Warner-Lambert's offer of a Spanish speaker in its toll-free information number for its pregnancy testing, e.p.t., should be the standard practice for any mass-market health product targeted to this age group.

Women bearing children, those choosing not to bear children, mothers raising children, and women who want to become pregnant all have special needs. Finding the right message and knowing how to deliver that message will be essential in the future as health-care providers work to revitalize a stable market.

Chapter 4

Marketing Family Products to Women: from Managed Care to Dr. Mom

He is thirtyish, handsome, and professional-looking. He's wearing chino pants, a polo shirt, and a pager attached to his trim leather belt. He is also a mamma's boy. "For 5 years, I suffered with heartburn. Finally, my mother made me see a doctor. He prescribed Zantac, and now my pain is gone."

Sons may grow up, leave home, and forget about their mother's birthday. But they're unlikely to forget about mom's health knowledge, as any mother whose adult son is suffering from a cold or the flu could tell you. The health expertise of mothers and other women is celebrated in advertising, such as the 1996 ad for Glaxo's Zantac in *Newsweek*, and confirmed by health marketers and other experts.

"Women want to be seen as equals, and we don't want to have these stereotypes—but it happens in my family, too," says Ann Boeke, director of corporate planning and development for Bellevue, The Woman's Hospital in Niskayuna, New York. "We carry babies. I think that bond continues. Maybe it is part of our nature to be nurturers."

Buying the family's health products and health insurance is one way women express their know-how. Women buy three out of every four drugstore products, which translates into a massive amount of spending. Sales of headache medication alone were $2.3 billion from June 1994 to June 1995, according to ACNielsen.

Women also spend billions on health insurance. They make about 40 percent of decisions about family health insurance on their own, while men make about 15 percent of the decisions on their own, according to focus groups conducted by women's health consultant Mary Anne Graf. Men and women working together make the remaining decisions. The health-insurance market included $110.4 billion in group premiums and $14.6 billion in individual and family policy premiums in 1992.

Everyone knows the importance of marketing family health products to women, but reaching women effectively is a more complicated task. For example, women's opinions about advertising are complex. Women respond positively to ads that portray a product or service helping their relationships with loved ones, says Kris Powell of the Anne Arundel Medical Center: "We tend to connect with life on a more personal level, so we have a tendency to personalize issues and experiences."

Yet some women are offended by constant references to the mother-child bond in health advertising. "You can't just market to women as caregivers of children," says Leslie Wolfe of the Center for Women Policy Studies. "You have to market to women as decision-makers for the family and as people who have care needs of their own. I think it is old fashioned and somewhat offensive when this is the only image we see."

About 80 percent of women believe that advertising never shows home life the way it is, according to a 1995 study by Grey Advertising. Seven in ten women say that advertising insults their intelligence. So even if women are focused on relationships, health advertising that portrays chirpy wives, glamorous mothers, and simplistic messages is likely to turn off the most important customers.

Whole segments of health care have failed to reach women in the past, experts say. "HMOs are way behind hospitals in marketing to women," says Sally Rynne. "HMOs are just now discovering that they have a market outside the employer."

Health marketers who target women as the family buyer must segment their audience based on the nature of the product, the age of the buyer, and the changes affecting American women. Family buyers come in all ages and configurations, from single never-married women purchasing arthritis medication for their mothers to single mothers purchasing cough drops for their children. Each segment has changed considerably and will keep changing in the future. Here are some of the most important trends:

- *Mothers are out of the house and older.* In 1994, American women were most likely to give birth between the ages 25 and 29. In 1970, women aged 20 to 24 had the highest birth rate. Mothers are also more likely to be in the work force than they were in the past—76 percent of married women with children aged 6 to 17 were in the work force in 1994, compared with 39 percent in 1960. Marketing

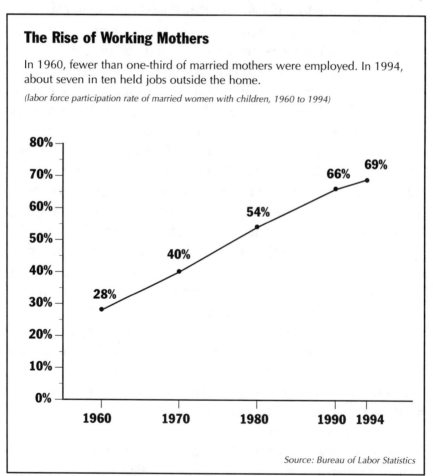

The Rise of Working Mothers

In 1960, fewer than one-third of married mothers were employed. In 1994, about seven in ten held jobs outside the home.

(labor force participation rate of married women with children, 1960 to 1994)

Source: Bureau of Labor Statistics

efforts for children's health products (such as cough medicine) and services (such as pediatric care) must be geared to mothers who work and targeted to appeal to women who are pressed for time.

- *Single mothers are everywhere.* The percent of children under age 18 living with their mothers alone increased from 11 percent in 1970 to 23 percent in 1994 among all Americans, and from 30 percent to 53 percent among black Americans. Moreover, the number of single-mother households is expected to increase steadily between 1995 and 2010, according to the Census Bureau, while the number of married-parent households declines. Advertising that

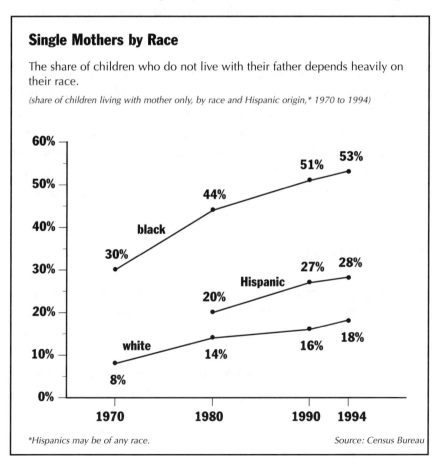

Single Mothers by Race

The share of children who do not live with their father depends heavily on their race.

(share of children living with mother only, by race and Hispanic origin,* 1970 to 1994)

*Hispanics may be of any race.   *Source: Census Bureau*

shows images of two-parent families will seem unrealistic to most young African-American families, and also to a high proportion of Latino and non-Hispanic white parents.

• *Mothers stay in charge of the household longer.* Job instability, divorce, and social changes are leading more adult children to live at home. Half of men aged 20 to 24 lived with their parents in 1993, and 10 percent of men in their 30s still lived with mom and dad. Overall, about one in ten adults aged 25 to 34 still lives with their parents, compared with one in 13 in 1980. With the "kids" still at home, older mothers are more likely to continue buying athlete's-foot remedies, acne medication, and other medical products for young adults.

• *Baby boomers are champion caregivers.* The aging of this massive generation will cause a rapid increase in the number of adults aged 45 to 64 in the next decade. These are the peak years of caring for an older parent. Expect to see more older Americans living into their 80s and 90s and more baby-boom women caring for and shopping for their elderly parents. Women spend much more time than men caring for older parents. Savvy marketers of products and services for the elderly focus their messages on middle-aged women.

It's Her Responsibility

The changing profile of American women creates a moving target for marketers. To see how far the market has moved, just look at the way advertisers have appealed to a woman's sense of responsibility for her family over the years.

Women of the 1920s were told bluntly that they were responsible for keeping their families healthy, says Anne Wehr, archivist of the American Advertising Museum in Portland, Oregon. Contemporary health advertising carries the same message in more subtle ways.

Women of the 1990s are busy with work and other responsibilities, so they do not respond to ads that imply they are bad mothers if their children get sick. Advertisers now aim for a balance. They attempt to appeal to women without forcing them to fill a traditional role.

This can be seen vividly in what Wehr calls "night-time dramas," an established genre of television commercial in which a woman quickly solves a family member's cough or cold problem using her superior health knowledge and the advertised product. "It's a form of power," says Wehr. But it is also a traditional role, repackaged for the working wife of the 1990s who needs precious sleep.

Though most women are in the work force and men have assumed more family duties, women still are expected to know what to do when a family member gets sick. "Women are doctors to men," says Ethel Klein, Ph.D., a market researcher in New York City and president of EDK Associates. "Going to the doctor has definitely remained her bailiwick." Women in Klein's focus groups tell her they even ask their own physicians about their husband's health problems, because the men are so lax about seeing a physician.

Marketers who want to appeal to working-age women must make their messages seem fresh and appealing to a sophisticated group of customers. Successful marketing to this group should:

- Acknowledge women's health knowledge;
- Know when women want to save money, and when trust or quality is more important;
- Promote the time-saving elements of products and services; and,
- Give women many options to learn about products.

The task of acknowledging women's health expertise while not portraying them as domestic servants is tricky. One product that excels at this mission is the cough medicine Robitussin, with its "Dr. Mom" campaign.

Mother Knows Best

Dressed casually in a cotton sweater, clutching a bottle of Robitussin in one hand and a dose of the medicine in the other, the woman in the Robitussin advertisement is a vision of maternal competence. The caption in a 1995 advertisement in *Ladies Home Journal* reads, "No One Has Made More House Calls." It includes the familiar Robitussin tagline: "Recommended by doctors, pharmacists, and, 'Dr. Mom'."

Many companies have turned to women physicians for advertising endorsements, but the "Dr. Mom" ads by A.H. Robins acknowledge the everyday healing efforts performed by mothers in the home. The campaign fits perfectly with the psyche of many mothers, says Mickey Smith, Ph.D., Barnard Professor of Pharmacy Administration at the University of Mississippi. "It positions mom as the person in charge of the family. Who would not buy a product from a company that recognizes your expertise?"

"When you're a mom, you hear, 'That's me.' The ad validates moms," says Kathleen Lewton of Porter/Novelli in Chicago. Mothers often hold different health standards for themselves and their children. This can be seen in the way women purchase store brands, such as the Equate pain relief product sold by WalMart. "Women will buy a store brand analgesic for themselves," says Smith, who has been a consultant for WalMart. "But when it comes time to buy for their kids, they'll go for as much information, safety, and confidence as they can get. That usually means a brand-name product."

Women are particularly cautious about anything taken internally by children, says Mark Edgar of *Private Label* magazine. "If they're going to save money and cut corners, they will try it on themselves, not on their children."

Marketers of store brands face a challenge in persuading customers to buy lower-priced items. Store brands typically offer samples and lower prices for children's health products to encourage parents to buy. "Once they try it and find out it's not going to hurt the child, they try it again," says Edgar.

Brand-name marketers of children's health items continue to focus on quality and trust, the paramount concerns for women buying children's products. Becton-Dickinson sells its fever thermometer with the tagline on its packaging, "First in quality since 1897." The product does little advertising but has a substantial share of the market, according to Chris Gallagher, associate product manager for fever measurement at the company's headquarters in Franklin Lakes, New Jersey.

Money Talks

Saving money plays a much greater role in women's health purchases that do not directly involve children. For example, women shopping for health insurance care more about having inclusive coverage for almost every procedure than they do about any other factor, including which doctor or hospital a plan uses. "Health-insurance coverage is far more important than anything else a woman could consider," says Mary Anne Graf, who draws her findings from focus groups of women conducted across the United States. "In most of our [focus groups], this factor is 10 or 15 times more important than anything else."

Kathleen Lewton sees a similar emphasis on health-insurance prices in focus groups of men and women in Utah. "The conventional wisdom—the myth—is that people are more concerned about quality and choice of physician," she says. But research shows that many women care far more about the cost of health care than about maintaining their physicians.

The emphasis on cost savings reflects the importance of financial constraints in women's lives. "Women only have one uterus, but they balance the household budget every month," says Graf.

Women are often reluctant to talk about the price of health care. "A lot of men have a deep suspicion of medical providers and hospitals, and they have no problem saying price comes first," says Graf. Women, she says, "are not willing to talk about price."

Insurance marketing also must be targeted to regional preferences. In some areas, such as New York City, women still maintain a preference for their own physician over cost savings, says Lewton. Random-sample surveys and focus groups of local women are often the only way to determine what means the most in a given market.

Marketing Time

Time is even more precious than money to many working mothers. Because so many mothers work, their time to shop and manage a household often cuts into the time they want to spend with their children. "Probably one of the biggest hurdles you face in marketing to women is getting them to pay attention," says Lewton. "Whether [women] are in the home or working outside the home, there's a time issue."

Direct mail and newsletters are one way to attract the attention of busy women. So is putting the issue of time-saving out front in marketing everything from health insurance to cough medicine.

The challenge of obtaining a timely doctor's appointment has been confounding both women and men for decades. "The thing I hear most consistently with women is, 'I can't even get in to see the doctor,'" says Graf. Health insurers with physicians who provide evening or weekend hours would do well to promote this access during enrollment time, when health plans can be changed.

Flexible appointment plans for children can also boost the appeal of physicians and health insurers to women. A four-physician pediatrics practice in Brighton, New York, launched drop-in hours from 8:30 to 9:45 a.m. daily in 1993. The hours offer a working mother a chance to have her child examined before she goes to work, avoiding a day of worry and speeding the start of any medication. "If moms or dads have to go off to work, they will know if the children can go to school," says Diane O'Neil, office manager of Twelve Corners Pediatrics.

The success of the drop-in hours has been "overwhelming," according to O'Neil. "People love it." The drop-in period started out staffed by one physician, and more had to be added. The practice is now so popular that it no longer accepts new patients.

Another important consideration for women is the time they spend getting a doctor's appointment. When Harvard Pilgrim Health Care, New England's largest managed-care plan, began advertising directly to women in 1995, it focused on a time-saving benefit. Women in the plan now can call an obstetrician-gynecologist directly for an appointment, without having first to call their primary-care physician, as the plan required in the past. "Time starvation is the big issue for women," says Maryann Wattendorf, associate marketing manager for the company. Wattendorf hopes that women will be more likely to choose a health plan for their families if they can save time in making their own appointments.

Products for new mothers also must be marketed with an awareness of the extreme time demands on women with infants. Pregnant women are the best audience for advertising about products for babies, because new mothers have very little free time once the baby is born, says Jay Borneman, a Philadelphia-based vice president of Standard Homeopathic Company of Los Angeles. One of the company's best-selling products, Hyland's Teething Tablets, is marketed so pregnant women will remember them once the baby is born. The company runs advertisements in baby magazines and sponsors organizations that attract pregnant women, such as Lamaze childbirth education groups. Although Hyland is a homeopathic product, it is among the top-four teething products nationally.

Women are the primary buyers of the company's pediatric products. "Most of the over-the-counter drug decisions, especially for products that are innovative or novel like ours, are made by moms," says Borneman.

Certain pharmaceutical products are inherently more appealing to mothers who are run ragged during the day and are exhausted at night. The success of Procter & Gamble's Nyquil, a night-time cold and cough remedy, was used as an example of skillful marketing in Al Ries and Jack Trout's 1986 book *Positioning: The Battle for Your Mind*. Children's Nyquil shows a cherubic small child fast asleep in bed, a visual promise to parents of a good night's sleep confirmed by the clever name.

"Nothing that's in that (Nyquil) is not in other drugs," says Smith of the University of Mississippi. "But they were phenomenally successful because they called it that."

Another product that sells to a mother's need for sleep is Delsym, a 12-hour cough syrup manufactured by Fisons Pharmaceuticals. Mothers are more likely than fathers to see the virtues of the product after reading the label, says Judy Cometa, former senior marketing manager in the pediatric marketing department of Fisons. "A man looking at Delsym versus Robitussin [which lasts from 4 to 6 hours] would probably pick up Robitussin. A man's not going to sit and read the label. A woman will say, 'I wonder what the side effects are. I wonder what the dosing is.' That's because women tend to get up in the middle of the night [with sick children]."

Death of a Dinosaur

The hectic schedule of American mothers has lessened the appeal of special, mail-in offers and other product premiums. "I think that the 1990s woman doesn't want gimmicks," says Cometa. "That is why we had to get rid of Danny the Delsym Dinosaur."

Consumers received a dinosaur figure if they sent in UPC codes from the product. "That worked for an earlier mom who was home with the kids," says Cometa. "Today, it's about convenience. I want my kid to sleep through the night. They've got to take it, it has to taste good, and it has to be worth the money. Women don't care about Danny the Delsym Dinosaur anymore."

As mail-in premiums like Danny the Dinosaur are phased out, marketers must turn elsewhere to reach busy working women. Bristol-Myers Squibb has an elaborate site on the World Wide Web geared directly to women (http://www.womenslink.com). "Women's Link" is complete with abundant information about family health products. The site provides news about headaches through the "Excedrin Headache Resource Center," along with information about cold and flu season. It even gives news about women's basketball. The page bills itself as a safe haven for women: "Welcome to Women's Link, the place for women in the know. It's a library, a cafe, a wellness center, and a spa all in one. Cyberspace isn't a men's club anymore."

The extensive information about headaches available through "Women's Link" includes a question and answer section about headaches and the opportunity to "ask the headache specialist," a physician at a major New York City hospital.

The "men's club" reputation of the Internet is fading as use of electronic media expands. Health marketers will increasingly have access to working women through their computers. They already use the Web to reach many professional women where they work.

Toll-free telephone numbers are another time-saving way to reach busy women with health information. Rogaine, a Pharmacia & Upjohn, Inc. product that can prevent hair loss in some patients, is marketed to middle-aged and older women and men. The product featured two different toll-free lines for phone callers in its 1995 advertising. Operators for the men's and women's line offer different promotional materials and are instructed about the different attitudes men and women have toward thinning hair. "Men see hair loss as a common fact of aging. For women, it's a more devastating problem," says Steven Bradford, product manager for prescription Rogaine. The independent lines give Rogaine a chance to target callers and focus on what women are most likely to want from the product.

The Mature Family Buyer

Marketers can appeal to many of the same traits in older women that they use to reach younger women. These include a woman's pride in helping to care for her family's health, and her interest in learning new facts about health. But American women aged 65 and older who buy family products are different than other women, and marketers can also sell to these differences.

Elderly women are unlikely to be in the work force, so they are unlikely to be as pressed for time as younger women. Their reduced income and added health needs make saving money more important than saving time. Women aged 65 and older are:

- *Big spenders on health care.* Americans aged 65 and older are just 13 percent of the population, but they spent 32 percent of all U.S. health dollars in 1994—including an average of $541 a year on prescription and over-the-counter drugs for each elderly household. Cost savings on drugs and other health products mean more to older Americans because they spend more than younger Americans on these goods. Households headed by Americans aged 25 to 34 spent an average of just $138 on drugs in 1994.

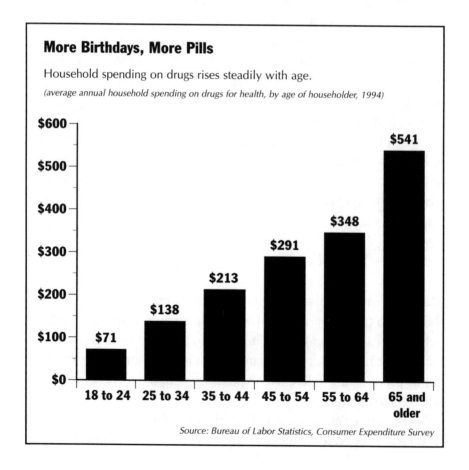

More Birthdays, More Pills

Household spending on drugs rises steadily with age.

(average annual household spending on drugs for health, by age of householder, 1994)

18 to 24	$71
25 to 34	$138
35 to 44	$213
45 to 54	$291
55 to 64	$348
65 and older	$541

Source: Bureau of Labor Statistics, Consumer Expenditure Survey

- *Traditional wives.* Women aged 65 and older are the last hold-outs of a more traditional era when divorce was rare, marriage was for life, and most women stayed home as homemakers. Only 6 percent of women aged 65 and older were divorced in 1994, compared with 13 percent of women aged 55 to 64 and 17 percent of women aged 45 to 54. Marketing messages that celebrate married life will affirm the life choices of a vast majority of older family health buyers.

- *Less educated than younger women.* Nearly 40 percent of women aged 65 and older did not graduate from high school, compared with 15 percent of American women aged 25 to 64. Marketers pro-

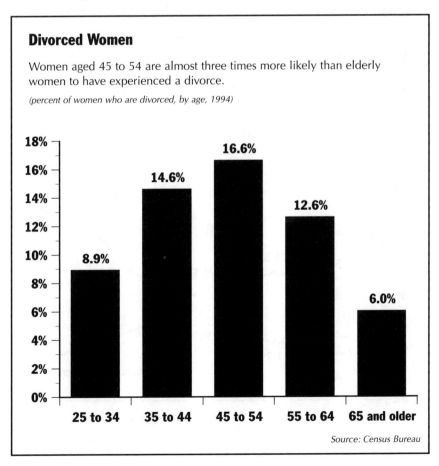

Divorced Women

Women aged 45 to 54 are almost three times more likely than elderly women to have experienced a divorce.

(percent of women who are divorced, by age, 1994)

Source: Census Bureau

moting health products or services to an older audience should steer clear of sophisticated data from clinical trials, unless their marketing is carefully targeted to more educated customers.

- *More likely to have vision trouble.* The small print typically included on drug labels, in drug advertisements, and in many brochures can be impossible for many older Americans to see. Large, clear print that includes good color contrast is essential in any marketing effort aimed at older Americans, men or women.

- *Less likely to use computers.* Older Americans are less likely to own home computers and therefore less likely to get information from

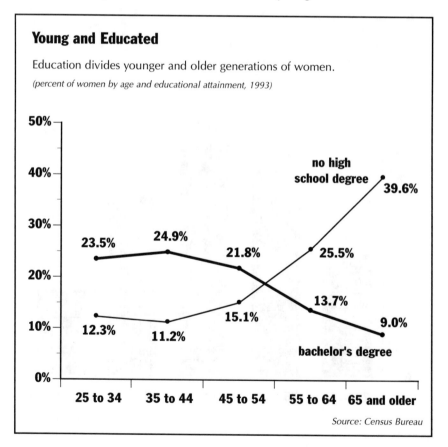

Young and Educated

Education divides younger and older generations of women.

(percent of women by age and educational attainment, 1993)

Source: Census Bureau

advertising sources such as the World Wide Web. Only 1 out of 10 Americans 65 or older owned a personal computer in the home in 1994, compared with 38 percent of Americans aged 30 to 49.

• *More likely to watch TV and read newspapers.* 40 percent of daily newspaper readers are aged 50 and older, compared with 29 percent of American adults aged 35 to 49, according to a 1990 report from Simmons. Half of all heavy television viewers were aged 50 and older. The company defines heavy viewers as individuals who watch at least 56 half-hour segments every two weeks.

Older Americans are also less likely than younger Americans to change television channels, and they are more likely to actually watch commercials, according to a 1994 study. This makes them prime audiences for health advertising on television.

Though older women may be the biggest health consumers, they traditionally have not been the focus of most health marketing. Yet several health companies now target older women as family buyers. Pharmacia & Upjohn, Inc.'s experience in marketing Rogaine suggests that older women can be a potent force in advertising products to men. While men are most likely to ask for men's information when calling the Rogaine hotline, women call both toll-free lines. Sometimes they ask for information about their own hair loss, but they often ask for information about hair loss for their spouses, says Bradford.

Another company that targets older women in its advertising for men is Merck, which launched a 1995 campaign for the prostate drug Proscar. In this case, women were a secondary target in ads addressed to men. Company officials counted on women to alert men to the problem once they saw the ads. "In general, men in this age group have a reluctance to recognize certain problems," says Merck spokesman John Bloomfield. "The advertising reflects the fact that women have a role to play in health-related decisions made by their spouses."

Efforts to appeal to women as family health buyers are fraught with complications and shifting boundaries. Over the next few decades, the older women's population will change as more independent, work-wise, mid-life women grow to maturity. The general population will also become more ethnically and racially diverse as younger Americans age. The youngest consumers of tomorrow will be different than those of the 1990s, with many more experiencing single-parent households and step-family relationships.

Successful marketers must be nimble in adapting to change and sensitive when trying to appeal to women as family buyers. A woman's sense of responsibility as a mother, wife, and daughter is likely to continue evolving. Meticulous targeting of specific health messages and careful market research will increase any company's odds of success.

Chapter 5

Higher Stakes, Hotter Debates: Marketing to Midlife Women

Ten years ago, many women under age 50 didn't know what osteoporosis was. Today, any woman who watches TV knows all about it. In late 1995, the approval of Fosamax launched a new wave of promotion and news stories about the degenerative bone condition that strikes older women. Fosamax was the first non-hormonal drug for osteoporosis sufferers, and Merck & Co., Inc. said the drug could help as many as 20 million American women.

The announcement was greeted with skepticism by some. The National Women's Health Network warned members that Merck was "inflating the need," and it advised women to consider alternatives to Fosamax that include exercise and improved nutrition. Such is the promise and the peril of marketing health products to middle-aged baby-boom women. This group blazed a trail of activism through health care in the 1960s and 1970s, and they are returning to their roots in the 1990s. "The 45-to-55-year-old woman is the one who brought Lamaze to America," says consultant Mary Anne Graf. "They are an aggressive group."

As the population of women entering menopause increases, midlife is emerging as a key area for health marketers. Sales of menopausal drugs are projected to increase from $1.4 billion in 1995 to $3.8 billion in 2000, with a compound annual growth rate of 23 percent, according to Find/SVP. Alternative therapies for menopause should also flourish as baby boomers enter this stage of life.

The menopause market was already crowded with new products and services by 1996, when the first baby-boom woman celebrated her 50th birthday. The number of women aged 45 to 54 is projected to increase 34 percent between 1996 and 2010, so the opportunities to serve this market will continue to increase exponentially.

Menopause is not the only health issue vexing middle-aged women. While most women aged 45 to 54 are generally healthy, they are at greater risk of developing cancer, heart disease, arthritis, and other serious ailments. Marketers of everything from vitamin supplements to mammography screening will have many potential customers in the next 15 years. But serving these customers will not be easy. Health products and advertising will be carefully scrutinized. Intense controversy over products (such as estrogen supplements) and services (such as osteoporosis testing) will continue as mid-life baby boomers seek a smooth transition through their menopausal years.

Using the "M" word

In 1996, Marie Lugano was shocked by a magazine advertisement for Neutrogena moisturizer. The tagline read "Menopause, daylight, and your skin." It was the first advertisement from a cosmetics company to appeal openly to middle-aged women by using the word menopause, says Lugano, president of the American Menopause Foundation.

The taboos surrounding menopause are just beginning to fall. Lugano has received letters berating her for including the American Menopause Foundation's name on the outside of an envelope. Cosmetics companies have consistently avoided using the "m" word. "The cosmetic industry doesn't want to have anything to do with this," says Lugano. But the sheer numbers of women entering menopause will encourage companies to break the silence.

Menopause is a process that lasts anywhere from a few weeks to more than five years, so it is difficult to gauge precisely how many women are experiencing it at any one time. Until recently, studies about menopause were limited. Yet the scope of the menopause market is clear. The menopause market is:

• *Constantly growing.* The number of women turning 51, the average age of the last menstrual period, will increase steadily from 1.4 million in 1996 to 2.2 million in 2015. This means that an average of 3,918 women turned 51 every day in 1996. By 2015, that will increase to 5,942 a day. The actual number of women experiencing menopause at any one time is larger than the number of women turning 51, because many women experience menopause for several years.

The largest estimates of the menopause market refer to every woman who has ever experienced menopause. This is a legitimate measure for products such as osteoporosis therapy and estrogen,

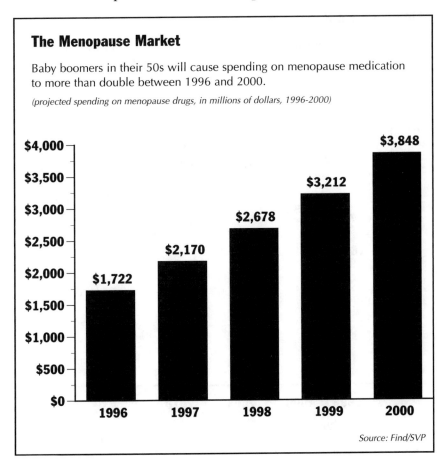

The Menopause Market

Baby boomers in their 50s will cause spending on menopause medication to more than double between 1996 and 2000.

(projected spending on menopause drugs, in millions of dollars, 1996-2000)

Source: Find/SVP

which can both be used throughout a woman's later years. In 1996, there were about 39 million women aged 50 and older. This number will climb steadily to 42 million by 2000, 46 million by 2005, and 61 million by 2020. But this larger group is not the true market for products sold during menopause.

• *Growing fastest to 2010.* The steady increase in the number of women aged 45 to 54 suggests that demand for products linked to menopausal changes will increase the fastest between 1996 and 2000. Over that five-year span, the number of women in this age

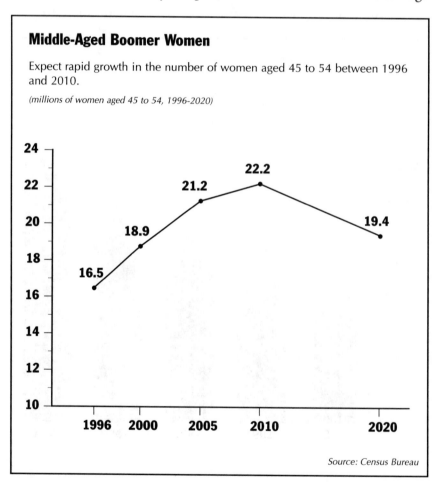

Middle-Aged Boomer Women

Expect rapid growth in the number of women aged 45 to 54 between 1996 and 2010.

(millions of women aged 45 to 54, 1996-2020)

Source: Census Bureau

group is predicted to increase 15 percent, from 17 million to 19 million. Between 2000 and 2005, the number of women in this group will increase another 12 percent, to 21 million. The years 2005 to 2010 will bring a 5 percent increase, to 22 million.

- *A during-and-after market.* Women experience menopause in two phases. The first phase includes symptoms, such as hot flashes, that occur during menopause. These symptoms can be treated with everything from hormone replacement supplements to ginseng pills. The second way that women experience menopause is as a process that changes their bodies. Some physical changes, such as vaginal dryness, may bother them throughout life. Others may make them more vulnerable to diseases such as osteoporosis.

- *Underserved.* Hormone replacement is the most widely prescribed therapy for menopause symptoms, but only about one in five menopausal women is involved because of widespread complaints about side effects and health concerns. New drugs may do a better job of meeting the need. In 1994, 19 drugs were in clinical trials to address everything from hot flashes to vaginal inflammation and dryness in post-menopausal women. But about one-third of menopausal women don't even talk to their doctors about symptoms, according to a 1993 survey. Marketers of new drugs and alternative therapies should find consumers eager for new options.

- *Willing to pay for relief.* Householders aged 45 to 54 are the biggest spenders and the biggest earners. Women in this age group are driving up sales of vaginal lubricants, books on menopause, and an explosion of new products that range from vitamin supplements to nutrition supplements derived from wild Mexican yams. Middle-aged women are also willing to travel to receive good medical care. Dr. June LaValeur, a physician who specializes in medicine for women over age 40, reports that her patients travel as far as 500 miles to see her.

• *Increasingly educated.* In 1994, nearly 85 percent of women aged 45 to 54 had a high school diploma, and 25 percent had a bachelor's degree or more. They are more likely to have a bachelor's degree than are women aged 55 to 64, of whom 19 percent have earned such a degree. Education increases a woman's appetite for information, and it also makes a woman more likely to ask questions of her doctor. Products and services that are backed up with well-organized, comprehensive information are more likely to gain their trust.

Middle Age Revisited

When an American woman reaches age 45, she is probably past the mid-point of her life. But the biological process of menopause is now often viewed as the start of the second half of a woman's adult life. Historically, the end of the childbearing years was seen as a time of loss. The first book written entirely about menopause, published in 1839 by C.F. Menville, explained the symptoms as a response to the death of the womb. In the early 20th century, menopause was viewed by physicians as "the death of the woman in the woman." As late as 1960, there was little medical research related to menopause, and the topic was rarely discussed in public. Women who suffered from hot flashes, night sweats, and insomnia tended to endure without relief.

The development of estrogen as a therapy for menopausal women in the 1960s was the beginning of menopause marketing. Estrogen was promoted heavily, and in some instances absurdly. The 1965 book *Feminine Forever* by Robert A. Wilson promised that women could look and feel youthful if they took estrogen for life. The product was advanced as a cure for everything from hot flashes to "menopause-related mental illness," a condition no longer considered legitimate.

When studies emerged in 1975 connecting estrogen to an increased risk of endometrial cancer, sales of estrogen supplements declined. Sales increased again in the 1980s with the discovery that estrogen combined with the hormone progesterone, could reduce the risk of endometrial cancer. The first U.S. menopause clinic was opened in Cleveland by Dr. Wulf H. Utian in 1982. A professional society devoted to the topic was founded in 1989, The North American Menopause Society.

Marketers in the 1980s began using celebrities to promote hormone replacement therapy. "We tried to find role models," says Helen O'Strowski, executive vice president at Porter/Novelli. "Everybody went through menopause, but nobody talked about it." Early advertisements for Ciba-Geigy's Estraderm used well-known women such as actress Shirley Jones.

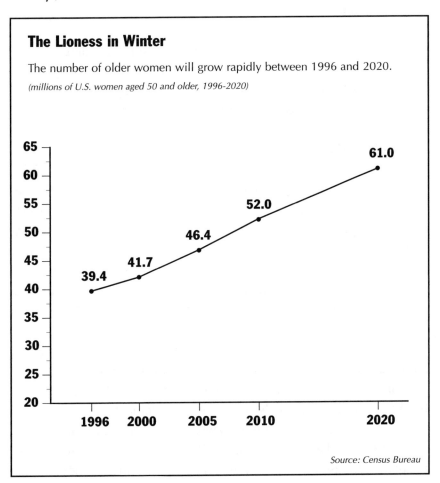

The Lioness in Winter

The number of older women will grow rapidly between 1996 and 2020.

(millions of U.S. women aged 50 and older, 1996-2020)

Source: Census Bureau

In 1992, Gail Sheehy's book *The Silent Passage* urged women to see menopause as "the gateway to a second adulthood." Sheehy and others wrote about health controversies surrounding the menopausal years, including the unknown health consequences of long-term estrogen use. In the mid-1990s, the quandary of whether to use estrogen supplements, commonly called hormone replacement therapy (HRT), has been complicated by research findings. Studies suggest that estrogen supplements reduce the risk of heart disease and osteoporosis but may also increase the risk of breast cancer.

As women struggle with the pros and cons of menopause treatments, they will demand three things:

- Accurate information about treatment options, including risk and benefit information;
- A sense of partnership with their health providers; and
- Alternate options for menopause-related problems.

Information Starved

Carol Landau, Ph.D., is one of the nation's leading authorities on menopause. As co-author of *The Complete Book of Menopause* (1994) and a clinical professor of psychology and human behavior at Brown University, she has been mulling over the needs of menopausal women for years. But when Landau presides over a "menopause town meeting" at a library or bookstore, she tries not to tell women what to do. She talks for a few minutes, then she lets audience members ask questions and listen to each other's experiences.

"The one thing menopausal women want is information," says Landau. "They want information, respect, communication, and partnership from their physicians. Women have been told that it's all in their head and it's all hormonal. Neither of these statements is true."

In a 1994 study, nearly 9 out of 10 women of menopausal age wanted reading material about menopause. Almost as many wanted to talk about menopause with a physician. Yet physicians often do not have the time or the inclination to tell menopausal women what they want to know. The study, which was conducted by the Harvard Community Health Plan, found that 56 percent of 180 physicians who saw menopausal women believed that HMO support of their practices for treatment of menopause was fair to poor.

Many physicians still fail to address the concerns of menopausal women. Osteoporosis, emotional well being, and heart disease are these women's greatest concerns, according to a 1993 Gallup poll of 833 women aged 45 to 60. Two-thirds of doctors discuss osteoporosis with these women, but only 52 percent talk about emotional symptoms and 46 percent talk about heart disease. Doctors are eager to discuss hormone replacement therapy; 84 percent of menopausal women report that their doctors raise the topic. But non-hormonal treatments such as exercise, diet, and stress reduction are recommended by less than 2 percent of doctors.

"Most women are saying the doctors aren't taking the time to answer their questions because doctors don't have the time," says Lugano, whose organization includes more than 250,000 women in support groups nationwide. "A lot of women are saying that their physicians don't have the time for anything except giving them estrogen and saying goodbye."

The prescribe-and-run routine is likely to offend baby-boom women. "Women aged 40 to 55 want to be a part of their health-care decision making," says Dr. LaValeur, a gynecologist with the Mature Women's Center at the University of Minnesota in Minneapolis. "They're tired of people telling them what to do. They want to know risks, benefits, and side effects."

Some physicians are serving women's yearning for information about menopause. Dr. Brenda Beeley, a homeopathic physician in San Rafael, California offers a six-hour class in menopause that attracts hundreds of women to each class. Beeley, an acupuncturest and herbalist as well as a homeopath, opened The Menopause Center in San Rafael, California in 1994. Many more physicians could gain an edge by providing more information. LaValeur's center has a library with videos, books, articles, and interactive computer programs about menopause and other women's health topics. Small discussion groups offer more information about specific topics.

Hospital programs about menopause have a wide appeal. They should continue to rise in popularity as more women approach menopause. Anne Arundel Medical Center sponsors four menopause education programs every year, and they are the hospital's most popular public offerings. Each program attracts between 100 and 200 participants.

"The interest in prevention [of menopause symptoms] and non-medical interventions is very high," says Kris Powell of Anne Arundel. Menopause seminars have helped the hospital build an image as a progressive and flexible leader in women's health. In 1996, the hospital presented a training session with one of the gurus of alternative menopause approaches, Dr. Christiane Northrup.

Innovative product marketers can also give menopausal women news about the subject. That is the strategy at Transitions for Health, a Portland, Oregon mail-order business that offers natural health products for menopausal women. The company has a site on the Internet that is staffed by a naturopathic physician (http://www.prog-est.com). Women can ask questions about menopause and have an answer delivered to them confidentially using e-mail. Sales have increased about 60 percent a year over the last three years. The company also offers information through its toll-free telephone number, a newsletter, and its catalog.

The most successful menopause product, hormone replacement therapy, also uses information-rich marketing. But the marketing of hormone replacement therapy also involves selling a palatable image of menopause to the public.

Marketing Estrogen

She is gray-haired and gorgeous. Reclining on a floral couch, relaxed and calm, with her aging golden retriever nearby, the woman is the picture of graceful middle age. "Menopause is one reason doctors prescribe

Premarin," the tagline reads. "Osteoporosis is another." Advertisements for Premarin, which had $850 million in sales and was the top-selling hormone replacement therapy product in 1995, have set a new pace for marketing to older women. Their images of attractive women, combined with information-packed copy, challenge the conventional wisdom that older women should not be shown in advertising.

The marketing of hormone replacement therapy is, in most ways, a spectacular success. Premarin is the number-one prescribed medication in the U.S., according to its manufacturer, Wyeth-Ayerst. Total sales of hormone replacement therapy are predicted to increase from $1.6 billion in 1996 to $3 billion in 2000, according to Find/SVP. A 1995 advertisement for Premarin reported that more than 8 million Americans take the drug.

Of course, there are more than 38 million women in the U.S. aged 50 and older. Resistance to the product is largely based on safety concerns. "Confusing messages are coming out of the scientific literature. They are driving women's concerns about the risk of breast cancer," says Bill Walker, marketing director for women's health products at Pharmacia & Upjohn, Inc., which makes Provera, a synthetic form of the female hormone progesterone. "I think women do not always understand the long-term benefits of hormone replacement therapy."

Most gynecologists favor hormone replacement therapy for many of their patients, according to a 1992 survey. But many women choose not to use the drug. In the Massachusetts Women's Health Survey, 9.3% of the 2,472 women of menopausal age used oral estrogen.

"[Women] don't get scared of heart attacks, and they should," says Landau. "They worry about breast cancer." Woman aged 75-to-84 are about ten times more likely to die of heart disease than breast cancer. But research indicating HRT's role in reducing heart disease are often overshadowed by studies that hint it could raise the risk of breast cancer. Side effects such as bleeding and headaches also discourage women from hormone therapy, says Lugano.

Marketing hormone replacement products is complicated and expensive. Wyeth-Ayerst, for example, publishes a bi-monthly magazine called *Seasons* for women taking Premarin. The magazine focuses on health, diet, exercise, and stress management issues. A group of pharmaceutical companies also published an eight-page guide called "Every Woman's Health in Menopause and Beyond" in a March 1996 issue of *Newsweek*. The guide says that hormone replacement therapy is an option "all menopausal women should ask their doctors about."

Such efforts can help women because of the tremendous need for accurate information about menopause, says Landau. But they will never convince the many women who will not consider hormone replacement therapy. "A whole group of women believe menopause is natural. They don't want to have anything to do with hormones," says Landau.

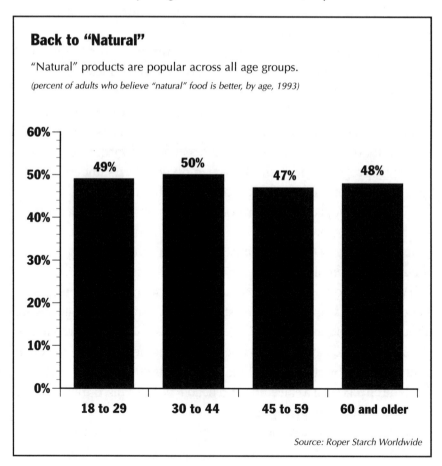

Back to "Natural"

"Natural" products are popular across all age groups.

(percent of adults who believe "natural" food is better, by age, 1993)

Age group	Percent
18 to 29	49%
30 to 44	50%
45 to 59	47%
60 and older	48%

Source: Roper Starch Worldwide

Younger baby boomers may be more likely than other age groups to choose "natural" options over synthetic ones. In 1993, 50 percent of consumers aged 30 to 44 agreed that "natural" food is better than other foods, compared with 47 percent of Americans aged 45 to 59 and 48 percent of Americans aged 60 and older, according to Roper Starch Worldwide. A widespread belief in the goodness of natural products could put hormone supplements off limits to a segment of the menopause market.

"People are afraid of estrogen. It doesn't work for everybody," says Brenda Beeley, who opened The Menopause Center because of the "hard push to synthetics." "Women really wanted to learn about alternatives." A large number of her patients are women who have never before tried alternative medicine. Beeley also publishes an alternative health-care journal called *MenoTimes.*

The quest for "natural" products and questions about the health risks linked to hormone replacement therapy will continue to limit the market until they are resolved. But these concerns could boost demand for Fosamax and the Sandoz nasal spray Miacalcin, a hormonal drug introduced in 1995 that previously was available only in injectable form.

Jump Start

The marketing of Fosamax, Merck's osteoporosis drug, relies on not-for-profit organizations, extensive advertising, and new technology. Months before the drug's approval by the Food and Drug Administration, Merck began an ambitious campaign to draw attention to women's risk of osteoporosis. Drug companies are not allowed to market drugs before they are approved by the FDA, but the Merck campaign raised awareness of the problem.

The company co-sponsored advertisements by the National Osteoporosis Foundation encouraging women to be tested for the disease. The campaign included a survey, which found that 60 percent of women did not realize they could be tested for early signs of osteoporosis using bone-mineral testing machines. The company also gave an educational grant to the Older Women's League, another not-for-profit group, to expand its efforts concerning osteoporosis. Merck's marketing was criticized in some circles, but most observers praised the pre-approval campaign. "How can there be too much attention to a disease that affects one-quarter of American women?" asks LaValeur. Once Fosamax was approved, Merck chose another controversial path by launching an extensive direct-to-consumer advertising campaign. The advertisements promote Fosamax, as a tool for independence and empowerment. One television ad shows an attractive woman in her 50s walking her dogs. "I couldn't believe it," the woman says. "Was I supposed to turn into a little old lady overnight, worrying about falling

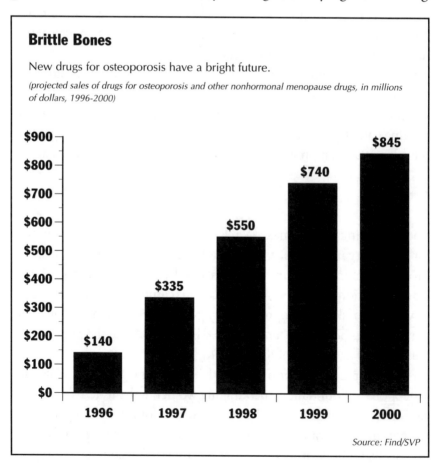

Brittle Bones

New drugs for osteoporosis have a bright future.

(projected sales of drugs for osteoporosis and other nonhormonal menopause drugs, in millions of dollars, 1996-2000)

1996	$140
1997	$335
1998	$550
1999	$740
2000	$845

Source: Find/SVP

down, breaking bones? Who has time to slow down?" The woman calls her doctor after hearing "something on the news," and discovers that there is something you can do about her problem. "Osteoporosis. I may have it, but it doesn't have me."

A Fosamax magazine advertisement opens with a picture of a lake and the text: "Since I found out about my osteoporosis, I've been afraid to walk to my mailbox when it rains." The ad exhorts women to "Fight your fear." Merck made an attempt to avoid scare tactics, says spokeswoman Maria Evans. "We know women don't want to be alarmed about another thing."

Marketers of another second-generation osteoporosis drug, Miacalcin, focus on education seminars for women and conventional public relations efforts rather than direct-to-consumer advertising, says spokeswoman Gina Moran at Sandoz, now Novartis.

One-half of all women and one in eight men are predicted to develop an osteoporosis-related fracture in their lifetime, according to the National Osteoporosis Foundation. The foundation predicts that as many as 25 million Americans already have osteoporosis. Moreover, women may lose up to one-quarter of their total bone mass within the first five years following menopause. That's why the future market for osteoporosis drugs looks strong. Sales should increase from $140 million in 1996 to $845 million in 2000, according to Find/SVP.

Selling a Test

Osteoporosis drugs are usually prescribed after the patient is given a test that measures bone density and the presence of the condition. Merck funds a program that will increase the number of bone density testing machines. The machines themselves also were extensively advertised. A 1995 ad showed one woman standing up straight and another woman with the characteristic dowager's hump of osteoporosis. "Women, don't let this happen to you," the advertisement said. The ads urge women to speak to their doctors about Osteomark (The NTx test), and they offer a toll-free number for information.

Presenting images of women crippled by osteoporosis is a risky move, says Landau. "Psychologically, I don't think it works. You respond to intense fear with denial and distance, not by wanting to learn more about the problem." But the overall marketing blitz is making a difference. Many osteoporosis screening programs had waiting lists in 1996. And doctors are increasingly likely to recommend osteoporosis testing to their patients, says Tillie Vastine, administrative director of The Women's Health Center of Allentown, Pennsylvania. "They have to. If they don't, they're going to be sued."

Osteoporosis may still be under-diagnosed, in part because the service is not covered by all insurers. Rochester (New York) Blue Cross-Blue Shield, for example, started covering screening in 1996. The company only intends to screen women with at least two risk factors, such as a family history of osteoporosis or a history of broken bones possibly linked to the disease, says Elaine Schaffer, a registered nurse with the medical affairs department.

The need for awareness of osteoporosis is universally acknowledged, but health marketers must be careful not to be perceived as pandering to women's fears. In September 1995, the National Women's Health Network warned members that osteoporosis drugs could be used in an unnecessary "mass medication of older women." Baby-boom women will reject over-ambitious claims for any medical products, so educational campaigns must prove the need for testing and medication.

Tummy Tucks and Face Lifts

Menopause isn't the only physical challenge faced by middle-aged women. As gravity takes its toll on once-taut flesh, women are more likely than men to take action. Almost 400,000 aesthetic plastic-surgery procedures were performed in the U.S. in 1994, according to the American Society of Plastic and Reconstructive Surgeons. About 350,000 of these, or 88 percent, were performed on women. Some 41 percent of aethestic plastic-surgery patients are aged 35 to 50, and 30 percent are aged 51 and older.

The marketing of cosmetic surgery is unique among medical fields. An advertisement for Dr. Charles D. Smithdeal in *Los Angeles* magazine says nothing about where Smithdeal went to medical school, but it does include a complete media history. "Dr. Smithdeal has been featured in *USA Today, Vogue, Cosmopolitan, Wall Street Journal,* and seen on "20/20" and "Inside Edition," says the ad. Above the copy is a photo of a voluptuous woman with a cascade of rich, dark hair. "Why are more women having breast implants today? Because the results are better than ever before," the 1995 ad promises.

Nowhere in medicine is there more of an emphasis on marketing than in the promotion of plastic surgery. It is characterized by effective and sometimes aggressive marketing, an increasing supply of patients, and a growing number of practitioners. For health marketers, cosmetic-surgery marketing can be seen as both a model of success and a cautionary tale.

Effective marketing is essential when patients pay out of pocket for services that are not medically necessary. "We are the one specialty where patients come to us wanting to have surgery," says Dr. Edward S. Truppman of Aventura, Florida, past president of the American Society of Plastic and Reconstructive Surgeons.

Educating potential patients is a critical part of marketing cosmetic surgery. This can be seen on the World Wide Web page produced by the American Society of Plastic and Reconstructive Surgeons and the Plastic-Surgery Educational Foundation (http://www.plasticsurgery. org), an electronic doctor referral center with connecting web sites for each participating physician. "It's a nice way to ethically present yourself," says Dr. Mark Jewell of Eugene, Oregon.

Jewell offers prospective patients a level of attentive communication unseen in most other specialties. When callers contact Jewell's office, the staff offers to send them brochures and other material about any procedure in which they are interested. Jewell makes himself and his staff available for about 45 minutes when potential patients visit for an initial consultation. He may show photos of his work or photos from a textbook. If prospective patients do not decide to have the surgery or do not contact the office after their initial visit, a staff member calls and asks if there is any other information they would like. "A lot of marketing in the past has played on insecurities," he says. Jewell adds that he prefers to focus on information.

Some cosmetic surgeons market themselves and educate their markets by offering public talks about cosmetic surgery at condominiums or other prime locations. Cosmetic surgeons may also promote themselves to beauty-parlor operators and people who run gymnasiums. These are "excellent sources of referral," according to Truppman. Good publicity can also benefit a practice. Truppman fondly recalls his own appearances on national television programs after he saved the life of a girl whose hand was bitten off by a shark. "We started an IV on the high seas," he says.

The more public face of cosmetic-surgery marketing is the heavy advertising seen in newspapers and magazines. Such marketing ranges from quietly informative to tasteless and misleading.

Many advertisements promise a better or more successful life through cosmetic surgery. An early 1990s ad for a New York practice of cosmetic surgeons featured the caption, "How Do You Stay Competitive in a World Where Youth Counts as Much as Experience?" A *Working Woman* article reported in 1994 that an early face-lift in the late 30s or 40s can contribute to added years of happiness. A 1996 ad in the Los Angeles magazine *Buzz* observes, "Nature has one opinion. You have another. We help you form it."

Such advertising offers high visibility and some hazards to cosmetic surgeons, says Truppman. Physicians who begin advertising before establishing a sturdy base of patients for referrals often find they can continue their practice only if they continue the high cost of advertising. Steady advertising can cost $200,000 a year or more, he says. Misleading advertising is another problem: some advertisements use photos that have been altered to show unrealistic before-and-after images, says Truppman.

Cosmetic surgeons also have been accused of over-marketing silicone breast implants. The implants were removed from the market for everyone but mastectomy patients by the FDA in 1993. Lawsuits from hundreds of thousands of women were largely responsible for the bankruptcy of Dow Corning Corporation in 1995. Public concern about the implants remains high, as 37,853 breast implants were removed in 1994.

Cosmetic surgeons bring some of their criticism upon themselves. A recent *Ms.* magazine story maligned the American Society of Plastic and Reconstructive Surgeons for stating in the early 1980s that women with small breasts suffered from a "disease" that could, presumably, be fixed by surgery. Such negative publicity is poison in a specialty dependent on the public image of its practitioners. Cosmetic surgeons must be scrupulously realistic in telling patients what surgery can and cannot accomplish, and in telling patients about potential risks as they are discovered.

The acceptance of marketing in cosmetic-surgery makes that specialty unusual in medicine. But the idea behind the marketing of cosmetic surgery can be applied to physicians in any competitive market. "Marketing helps you distinguish your practice from others," says Jewell. "It creates the perception of quality."

Emerging Markets

In the next 15 years, a wave of middle-aged women will create whole new industries in health care. "It's a marketer's dream," says Landau. "People want information and alternatives."

One product category that has flourished is sexual lubricants designed for women aged 45 and older, as more women who are likely to suffer from vaginal dryness remain sexually active. Sales of these products were estimated at $34 million in 1993, according to Packaged Facts. They will likely increase as the population ages.

Other products include mineral supplements, such as calcium to prevent bone loss; vitamins such as Vitamin E to prevent hot flashes; and various herbal and homeopathic medicines. The future for these alternative approaches should be bright as more baby boomers enter their menopausal years.

The market of menopausal women is not the easiest to reach, particularly for promoters of alternative health products, says Jay Borneman, of Standard Homeopathic Company. There's no commercial magazine strictly for menopausal women. *Modern Maturity*, the best-known older person's magazine, has strict limits on its health advertising. Television advertising is often too expensive.

Yet the market of women reaching and moving beyond menopause is one that Borneman and others will continue to pursue. Women will continue to search for alternatives without side effects for the menopausal symptoms that bother them. New drug products may present better alternatives to hormone replacement therapy. And the increasing national interest in alternative medicine suggests that many women will not choose drugs, even if they are better than the current choices. Marketers of conventional and unconventional products must be careful to provide enough product information to satisfy the demanding mid-life woman.

Chapter 6
Older Women, Greater Needs

G ripping her handlebars while pausing on the trail, the bicycle rider looks like any other athletic middle-aged woman. Her health problem—incontinence—is under control. "Your light bladder problem doesn't bother you much," says the 1996 ad for Stayfree Serenity bladder protection products. "Now it won't bother you at all."

Twenty years ago, incontinence was a silent problem with no commercial products offering a solution. Today, women's magazines and television portray older Americans who have found commercial solutions, and incontinence products are a huge industry. Sales hit about $1.1 billion in 1995, which was double the figure for 1988, according to the market research firm Frost & Sullivan.

The proportion of Americans aged 55 and older is increasing steadily. The number of women in this age group is predicted to grow 63 percent between 1996 and 2020, from 31 million to 51 million. Products and services for problems that range from incontinence to arthritis and heart disease will claim a bigger part of the health dollar. Most of the consumers will be women, because women generally live longer than men. But marketers still have a lot to learn about reaching older women. "I don't know of anybody that's really doing an effective job," says Frank Conaway, president of primelife, a marketing firm in Orange, California.

The distinctive nature of the older women's market calls for a careful review of the way they live, spend money, and form beliefs. The differences in lifestyle between a 58-year-old attorney with a touch of arthritis who scuba dives for pleasure and her wheelchair-bound 98-year-old mother with osteoporosis are nearly as great as the differences between infants and their mothers.

Illness and disease erase the differences between people. Everyone who feels pain wants relief, compassionate medical care, and a cure if possible. Suffering draws 58-year-olds and 98-year-olds together. But effective marketing to older women demands more than simply knowing what different groups of women need. "Need does not really mean want," says Margaret Wylde, Ph.D., president of the ProMatura Group of the Institute for Technology Development, a marketing consulting firm in Oxford, Mississippi. The challenge of influencing the "wants" of a mature woman depends on knowing what makes her different from her daughters and granddaughters.

Power in Numbers

Older women are almost invisible in the media. Unseen in most advertising and unnoticed for their accomplishments, they are outcasts from many aspects of American life. Yet in health care, older women are the most important market segment. Their abundant spending on health care sets them apart from other Americans. Mature women also are different because aging changes their attitudes toward health care. The messages health marketers send to older women must reflect these changes.

The health problems of age define this market. About 80 percent of heart-attack deaths are among people aged 65 or older, and about 77 percent of women with a new diagnosis of breast cancer are over age 50. Many of the problems common among older women, such as arthritis and high blood pressure, are treated with drugs that must be taken regularly for life. That is why elderly women are a key market for pain relievers and many other drugs.

The older women's market is:

- *The biggest-spending group for health services.* Mature women and men have similar health problems as they reach the end of life. But women live an average of seven years longer than men, so they are the most common face of the elderly health consumer. Men and women aged 65 and older spent 33 percent of all U.S. dollars on health care in 1994, for a total of $56 billion. Americans aged 65 and older also are the most frequent hospital visitors, claiming 48 percent of all days spent in a hospital in 1993. They also are heavy users of screening and preventive medical services, such as mammography.

- *Increasing steadily in size.* Overall growth in the number of women aged 55 and older is predicted to be moderate until the year 2011, when the largest segments of the baby-boom generation reach this

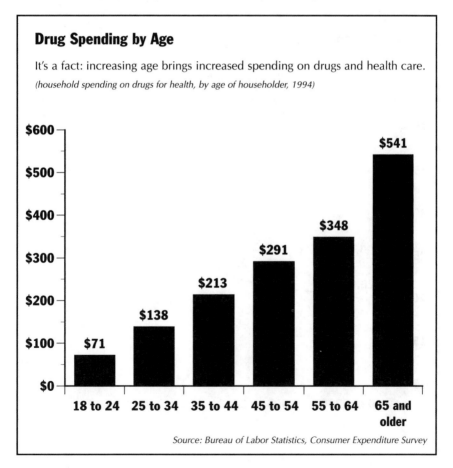

Drug Spending by Age

It's a fact: increasing age brings increased spending on drugs and health care.

(household spending on drugs for health, by age of householder, 1994)

Source: Bureau of Labor Statistics, Consumer Expenditure Survey

age. Between 2010 and 2020, the number of women aged 55 and older is expected to increase 25 percent, from about 41 million to 51 million, for an annual growth rate of 2.5 percent. Growth will slow down to 11 percent between 2020 and 2030, with the population of women aged 55 and older increasing from 51 million to 57 million.

- *Growing fastest in the oldest age groups.* Women are living longer because of medical advances and better preventive medicine, so the largest increases in population are projected to be among the oldest old. The number of women aged 85 and older should double between 1996 and 2030, from 2.7 million to 5.4 million. Dramatic

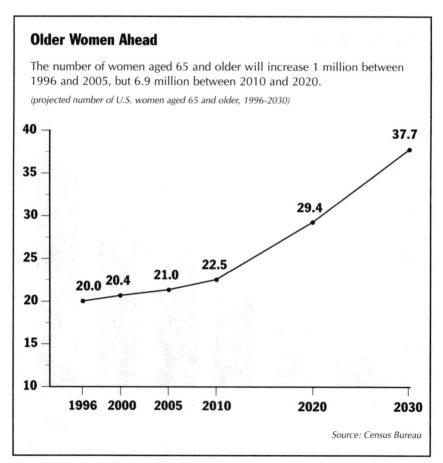

Older Women Ahead

The number of women aged 65 and older will increase 1 million between 1996 and 2005, but 6.9 million between 2010 and 2020.

(projected number of U.S. women aged 65 and older, 1996-2030)

Source: Census Bureau

increases should occur in the near future as well, with the number of women aged 85 and older increasing 26 percent from 1995 to 2005, to 3.4 million. Demand for home health care, nursing homes, and drugs for arthritis and other chronic problems will continue to increase rapidly.

- *Unique in how it responds to marketing.* The physiological changes associated with aging include greater difficulty distinguishing color contrast, hearing high-pitched tones, and reacting quickly to sensory stimulation. Marketing and other messages for older customers

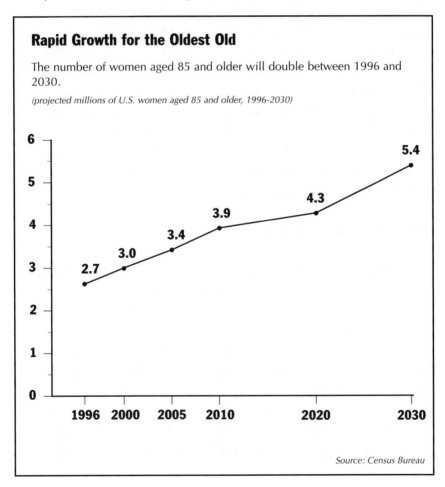

Rapid Growth for the Oldest Old

The number of women aged 85 and older will double between 1996 and 2030.

(projected millions of U.S. women aged 85 and older, 1996-2030)

Source: Census Bureau

should be simple and concrete, with no unnecessary information or nonsense syllables in copy, says Charles D. Schewe, Ph.D., professor of marketing at the University of Massachusetts in Amherst. Print media may be a better choice than television or radio because it allows consumers to pace themselves, says Schewe. Type size should be large, type style should be simple, and color contrasts should be obvious.

• *Less well-off than men.* Poverty is more familiar to older women than to older men. Fourteen percent of women aged 65 and older were living in poverty in 1995, compared with 6 percent of older men. Poverty is most common among older Hispanic women who live alone: 49 percent in this group lived in poverty in 1995. But most older women and men are not poor. In 1994, householders aged 55 to 64 spent more money, on average, than did householders aged 25 to 34. Most Americans spend freely on cosmetics, automobiles, clothing, and some forms of entertainment until their 70s. As women with workplace experience and higher education enter their mature years, the consumer power of mature women should increase, while their poverty rates decline.

From Doddering to Dynamic

On those rare occasions when older women appear in advertising, their image is usually out of date or unrealistic. Think of the aggressively antisocial character played by Clara Peller in Wendy's infamous "Where's the Beef?" commercial.

"Advertising still portrays older adults as less able than they are," says Margaret Wylde of ProMatura. "Many ads for health-care and pharmaceutical products are still condescending and inappropriate."

Wylde asked a national sample of 737 men and women aged 55 and older for their opinions of advertising geared to seniors. Certain types of advertising are particularly offensive to this group, she found. They despise advertising that is unrealistic or offensive, or ads that portray seniors in unappealing ways.

Direct references to age or to the unsavory details of health problems are offensive to many mature women. "I wouldn't discuss age in any way, shape, or form. I wouldn't dwell on the need that's being served," says Wylde. "Focus on the benefit of the product." For health marketers, this means showing what active mature women can do if they use a product or service. "Keep away from degrading the individual and reminding them that they have a need," says Wylde.

Mature women also dislike advertising that shows distasteful physical

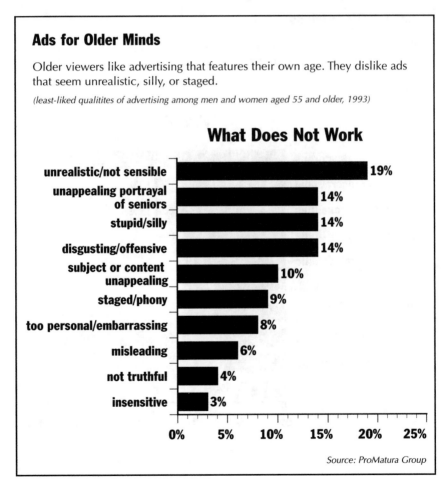

Ads for Older Minds

Older viewers like advertising that features their own age. They dislike ads that seem unrealistic, silly, or staged.

(least-liked qualitites of advertising among men and women aged 55 and older, 1993)

What Does Not Work

unrealistic/not sensible	19%
unappealing portrayal of seniors	14%
stupid/silly	14%
disgusting/offensive	14%
subject or content unappealing	10%
staged/phony	9%
too personal/embarrassing	8%
misleading	6%
not truthful	4%
insensitive	3%

Source: ProMatura Group

problems. Ethel Klein of EDK Associates advised Merck & Co. not to use the unsightly image of the so-called dowager's hump that occurs in women grossly disfigured by osteoporosis when it markets the drug Fosamax. "Part of what advertising sells is what women value about themselves," she says. "Women value self respect."

The best ads for seniors are humorous, says Wylde. Second best are ads that show older and younger people together, and ads that show older television personalities that strike seniors as realistic. "The way to target them is to use themes and actors that look like them and act like

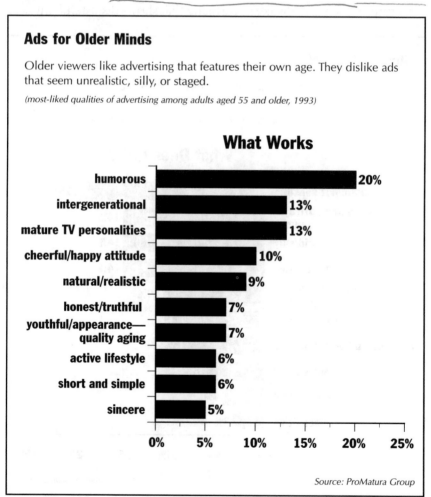

Ads for Older Minds

Older viewers like advertising that features their own age. They dislike ads that seem unrealistic, silly, or staged.

(most-liked qualities of advertising among adults aged 55 and older, 1993)

What Works

humorous	20%
intergenerational	13%
mature TV personalities	13%
cheerful/happy attitude	10%
natural/realistic	9%
honest/truthful	7%
youthful/appearance— quality aging	7%
active lifestyle	6%
short and simple	6%
sincere	5%

Source: ProMatura Group

them," she says.

Advertisers face many obstacles to understanding the mature market. The obstacles often come from within their own ad agencies, says Richard A. Lee, principal of High-Yield Marketing, a strategic marketing consulting group in Minneapolis-St. Paul, Minnesota. Three-quarters of the 206 advertising professionals Lee surveyed in 1994 greatly underestimated the high levels of discretionary spending among older Americans. Fifty-four percent believed the stereotype that seniors don't switch brands—an assumption that has been proven to be untrue.

Ignorance and bias about the mature market cause lost opportunities, says Lee. "We stop treating people as consumers and start treating them as dependents at a surprisingly early age."

One way to market more effectively is to target messages to specific groups. "When people say, 'We're marketing to people over 50,' I say, 'How much money do you have?'" comments Conaway of primelife. "You're talking about the world. You have to segment." Knowing how to divide the mature women's market can make the difference between success and failure.

Market Surgery

Disease and illness drive the market for health care. People who know they have heart disease are the market for heart surgeons and drug companies. But health marketing is far more complicated than selling light bulbs or milk. Many health marketers say they are really in the business of education.

Many women with health problems don't know they have them, or they do not realize medical help could ease their problem. In 1993, 45 percent of women aged 50 and older did not get an annual mammogram. Half of people with urinary incontinence don't seek help from a physician, although this problem can be treated effectively most of the time. Health marketers often must target groups of women at risk and tell them about the signs and symptoms of a problem before they bring up the subject of treatment.

The mature women's market for health care can be approached in four different ways. It can be segmented by disease or illness, by life experience, by racial or ethnic identity, and by age.

Targeting women who are aware of their health problem is the most common form of market segmentation. But lifestyle differences are also effective ways to divide mature women into market segments. Hospitals have devised programs for women who have lost a spouse, or for those who care for an older parent or spouse, says consultant Ruthie Dearing. Offering support to women during a difficult transition is one way to forge a relationship that may pay off in the future.

The oldest Americans are the least ethnically and racially diverse age group, but this will change. Eighty-five percent of Americans aged 65 and older were non-Hispanic whites in 1996, compared with 71 percent of baby boomers (aged 32 to 50) and 66 percent of children (under age 19). But reaching older minorities is already important in some markets. For example, an estimated 51 percent of New Mexico state residents are of Hispanic origin, as are 28 percent of Californians. Western marketers who blanket the mature women's population with a single message will miss out on the increasing number of older Americans who read only Spanish newspapers and watch only Spanish television.

Age may only be a state of mind, but it does play a key role in determining the health products and services women want and need. It is useful to divide older women into three age and activity groups.

The Youngest Old. Women aged 55 to 65 are at some risk of arthritis, breast cancer, and heart disease, but they are still likely to be leading active and vigorous lives. These women are more likely to be better-educated and to have earned more money on their own than have older women aged 65 and older. "Women aged 54, 55, and even 60 have been working most of their lives," says Frank Conaway of primelife. Women in this group respond to marketing aimed at busy people, such as mammogram facilities that offer quick service and exercise classes to help prevent heart disease. About 60 percent of 55-to-59-year-old

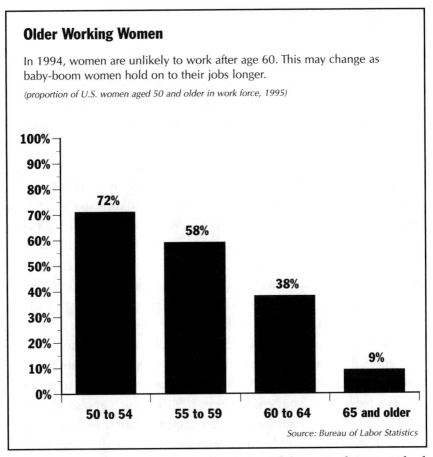

Older Working Women

In 1994, women are unlikely to work after age 60. This may change as baby-boom women hold on to their jobs longer.

(proportion of U.S. women aged 50 and older in work force, 1995)

Source: Bureau of Labor Statistics

women still worked in 1995, but a majority of those aged 60 to 64 had either retired or were not working. In the future, most of the youngest-old women will still be working, making them accessible to marketers through workplace health promotion and company newsletters.

Aging But Active. The middle group of mature women, most commonly aged 65 to 75, may still be leading active lives—but health is a greater concern. Heart disease is the leading killer of women over age 65, and by age 70 the incidence of Alzheimer's disease increases dramatically. Women aged 65 to 74 are still most likely to live with a spouse and be in good health. In 1991, about 74 percent of all Americans aged 65 to 74 said they were in good to excellent health. Only 1 percent of people aged 65 to 74 lived in nursing homes in 1990.

Aging but active women are generally active consumers. They are a major market for health products and services that enable women to remain healthy and active, including osteoporosis medicine, vitamin supplements, and heart-healthy eating and cooking programs. Medical advances are likely to continue boosting the activity and independence level of women in this age group.

Oldest But Diverse. Women aged 75 and older are a diverse group, including world-traveling 80-year-olds and 98-year-olds in nursing homes. All women aged 75 and older have a high likelihood of being widowed, and most women in this age group live alone. Yet many continue to feel well and stay active. In 1991, 66 percent of all Americans aged 75 and older reported that they were in good to excellent health. Independence becomes a primary concern among the oldest group, as health problems become more threatening. Heart disease and bone fractures due to osteoporosis become much more common among women aged 75 and older. Women in this group also dominate the population in nursing homes. Yet even among people aged 90 to 94, only one in three lived in a nursing home in 1990. Products and services that enable women to remain independent appeal strongly to women aged 75 and older. These include transportation services to doctors' appointments, drugs that enable them to fend off illness, and vitamins to keep them energetic.

There is no magazine for women aged 75 and older, and no television program for women aged 55 to 64. Yet there are many opportunities to segment older women by age. The bike rider advertisement for Stayfree Serenity pads shows that incontinence can be a problem even for women in their 50s. The image of a younger, active woman is appropriate and appealing to busy 55-to-64-year-olds. Collecting information on the ages and activity levels of health-care consumers will become more critical to marketers in the future, as the mature market grows and becomes more diverse.

Hospitals and Healing Hearts

The ultrasound photo is cloudy, but the caption makes the subject clear. "A Woman's Heart Has Loved, Been Broken and, Until Now, Pretty Much Ignored in Research." Not anymore, promises the 1996 advertisement for the Women's Heart Center at the University of Pittsburgh Medical Center. "What it comes down to is a woman's heart needs special care," the ad says. "But if you're a woman, you've always known that."

Older women patients were once the bedrock of a flourishing hospital system. Few efforts had to be made to draw them in to the hospital. But as hospital competition increases and managed care continues to force cost-cutting, marketing aimed at older women should become more common. Nearly 500 community hospitals closed between 1972 and 1992, and more closings are expected.

Hospitals that are struggling to remain open must focus on their best customers, and that means seeking out older women as inpatients, outpatients, and sources of referrals. Older women's health needs are immense, and their hospital stays tend to be long and expensive. In 1993, 1.4 million women aged 65 and older were discharged from hospitals for reasons related to heart disease, with stays averaging seven days. Another 402,000 women were discharged after cancer-related stays averaging 8.6 days, and 381,000 were released after treatment for bone fractures so serious they required average stays of 9.3 days.

Just as hospitals market to younger women well before labor and delivery begins, they must reach out to older women before they are rushed to the hospital with a broken bone. Hospitals that attract older women through health clinics, exercise classes, or free information about incontinence will have an advantage over those that wait to show their mettle in an emergency. The importance of preventive health measures in reducing heart disease, cancer, and other diseases also provides great opportunities for hospitals to educate older women and earn their appreciation.

Different groups of mature women have different expectations about health care. For example, older women generally do not seek the type of partnership many younger women want with a physician. Mature women are more likely than younger women to trust their physicians, says consultant Ethel Klein. "They're used to a different kind of provider—one who is paternalistic," says Dr. June LaValeur. For this reason, marketing that promotes changing values and ideas in health care is more likely to be threatening than promising to this group. Marketers of health maintenance organizations for seniors would be better off stressing the familiar, steady aspects of their physicians and health networks.

Promoting the presence of women physicians is unlikely to make a difference to older women, because this group generally does not care if a gynecologist is male or female, according to a 1992 study by The Gallup Organization, conducted for Mycelex-7. The study found that 18 percent of women aged 50 and older preferred a female gynecologist, compared with 34 percent of women aged 18 to 49. Almost two-thirds of women aged 50 and older had no preference for a male or female gynecologist, compared with fewer than half of women aged 18 to 24.

In an effort to reach older women early, some hospitals have launched what at one time was the unthinkable: medical clinics for the elderly. Conventional wisdom says that women do not want to be told they are

Who Wants a Woman Doctor?

Most women don't care if their doctor is a man, but younger generations are more likely to prefer a woman.

(percent of U.S. women by physician preferred, by age, 1992)

	prefer female	prefer male	no preference
18 to 24	34%	14%	49%
25 to 34	34	15	51
35 to 49	34	10	56
50 and older	18	13	65
total	28	13	57

Source: The Gallup Organization

old. But the Mature Women's Center at the University of Minnesota in Minneapolis offers a new kind of health care for older women who are willing to face their special health needs. The center, designed for women over age 40, offers primary medical care, osteoporosis testing, and classes to help women quit smoking.

One problem for many older women is finding transportation to their medical care, says LaValeur, a gynecologist at the center. Older women may not know how to drive, may not own a car, or may not feel comfortable navigating public transportation or driving due to physical problems. Social workers at the Mature Women's Center arrange transportation for patients in need of help.

Physician services to older women can also be promoted through hospital newsletters. When urogynecologist Gunhilde Buchsbaum arrived at Highland Hospital in Rochester, New York, her program on urinary incontinence was promoted in an article she wrote on the topic in the hospital's women's center newsletter.

Scheduling programs at times that are convenient for older women is also essential. Older women who do not work are unlikely to attend evening health programs, says Dearing, "because they don't like to go out at night." But women who are still in the workplace may only attend weekday health programs if they are offered at night.

Fitness classes for seniors promote the two women's health centers linked to Bellevue, The Woman's Hospital in Niskayuna, New York. Classes have opened hospital doors for some women. "What often happens is women come for exercise," says Ann Boeke, director of corporate planning and development for the hospital. "Pretty soon they're saying, 'Can I come here for a mammogram? I don't have a doctor'." Weight-bearing exercise is now seen as a critical part of osteoporosis prevention, so exercise classes should hold an increasing appeal to women.

When a hospital promotes itself as a fitness and exercise champion, its role in the community changes. Many older women go to their local hospital to take a class and meet friends. "They do yoga and tai chi," says consultant Mary Anne Graf. "The hospital functions almost as a senior citizen center."

This repositioning could have a big payoff for a hospital. If women who take yoga in the hospital choose physicians and managed-care plans linked to the hospital when they need medical care, the hospital gains market share. The idea is to send a message that older women are important and matter to the hospital.

Arthritis Explosion

More than 23 million women suffer from arthritis, and this group should increase dramatically in the future. Arthritis is already a key area for marketers of health products and services for older Americans, and the time is right to prepare for new competition as the market expands.

McNeil Consumer Products, a division of Johnson & Johnson, changed the arthritis market when it launched Arthritis Foundation Pain Relievers in 1994. *Consumer Reports* maligned the brand for charging more than necessary, even though the company made clear that part of the purchase price went to research and support for the Arthritis Foundation. Others criticized the non-profit foundation for lending its name to a commercial product. Officials at the Arthritis Foundation replied that the partnership was absolutely necessary. "We see this as literally the epidemic of the future," says Eric Hargis, executive vice president for the Atlanta-based foundation. "As many as 60 percent of people with arthritis do not receive appropriate treatment, based on the perception that there's nothing you can do about it. These are staggering numbers, and we can't reach them on our own."

The number of women with arthritis is expected to increase from about 23 million in 1989-91 to 29 million in 2005 and 36 million in 2020. Nearly all of the growth is predicted to occur among older women. By age 65, the majority of women suffer from some arthritis. Women are more likely to develop arthritis than men; 17 percent of all women have arthritis, compared with 12.5 percent of men. "Arthritis is inevitable for most women," says David Williams, a principal in The

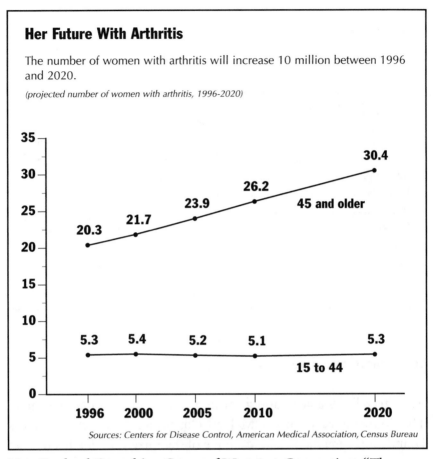

Her Future With Arthritis

The number of women with arthritis will increase 10 million between 1996 and 2020.

(projected number of women with arthritis, 1996-2020)

Sources: Centers for Disease Control, American Medical Association, Census Bureau

New England Consulting Group of Westport, Connecticut. "The market is big, and it's going to get bigger."

The prevalence of arthritis varies from state to state, depending largely on the age structure of the population. In Florida, arthritis already affects one in five residents. By 2020, it is predicted to affect one in four. But in youthful Alaska, only one in ten residents currently suffers from arthritis, and this figure is not predicted to change much in the future.

Arthritis therapies are certain to receive more attention as women eager to remain active seek pain relief and cures. But these products and services will also be under increasing scrutiny as younger, more educated women develop the disease.

States of Arthritis

One in five Florida residents had arthritis in 1990. In 2020, it will be one in four.

(states with highest percentage of population with arthritis, and thousands of cases, 1990, and projected to 2020)

	1990		2020	
	cases	percent	cases	percent
Florida	2,471	19.1%	4,803	24.7%
West Virginia	331	18.2	394	21.3
Arkansas	417	17.5	646	21.5
Iowa	485	17.0	607	20.0
Alabama	679	16.7	1,037	19.8
Missouri	870	16.7	1,225	20.0
Tennessee	823	16.7	1,345	20.1

Sources: Arthritis Foundation, Center for Disease Control

Competition and Giveaways

Arthritis relief is a large and growing market, but it's not a sure thing. The Johnson & Johnson McNeil-Consumer Products Arthritis Foundation agreement is an example of the mixed results this market can offer. For the Arthritis Foundation, the agreement has resulted in more members, increased visibility, and more cash for research. The Foundation is expected to receive its second $1 million check at the end of 1996 through an agreement that guaranteed it a minimum contribution and protected it from risk if the brand was unsuccessful.

For Johnson & Johnson, the results are more difficult to gauge. The company reportedly spent $30 million to launch the product, a sum including $16 million for advertising and funding for 30 million samples. McNeil, which refused to comment on the product, is one of many companies that have struggled in the increasingly competitive market for arthritis pain relief. "Probably right now all the manufacturers of over-the-counter analgesics are not thrilled with net profits," says Hargis of the Arthritis Foundation.

Sales of over-the-counter analgesics for arthritis dropped between 1993 and 1994, from $135 million in 1993 to $115 million in 1994, according to Kline & Company, Inc. in Fairfield, New Jersey. Sales of general pain killers for adults, which are also used by people with arthritis, increased only slightly during that period, from $2.6 billion to $2.7 billion.

Several factors have made this business more competitive, including many new prescription and over-the-counter products introduced in the 1990s. One report says that more than 400 pain relievers entered the market between 1983 and 1994. New products are doing well. Sales of Aleve, a form of the prescription drug Naprosyn, increased 54 percent between 1995 to 1996. But older brands saw sales decline during the period: Tylenol sales were down 4 percent, and sales of Bufferin went down 19.2 percent.

Technology also is driving competition in the market, as new products are developed that offer pain relief for half a day or more. Conventional pain relievers such as Arthritis Foundation acetaminophen face competition from drugs such as Relafen, a prescription drug product that lasts 12 hours and has been heavily advertised.

The current marketing of arthritis drugs wisely shows few if any of the disfigurements linked to severe arthritis. Instead of gnarled hands, a magazine ad for Relafen shows an immaculately clean ceramic bathtub glimmering in the morning light. "Arthritis pain can turn this into a morning workout," says the ad.

Sales of SmithKline Beecham's Relafen increased 52 percent in 1994, thanks to a technique that could be termed the Santa Claus strategy. Callers to the company's toll-free number in 1996 received a bounty of material, including a ten-minute video about living with arthritis, a booklet recapping the information in the video, a guide for talking to physicians about arthritis, and a booklet about Relafen.

Callers also are invited to join Relafen's Positive Steps club when they receive their first prescription. Membership includes a free six-month subscription to *Health* magazine and a free six-month membership in the Arthritis Foundation. While such marketing efforts are expensive, they also give the company a lasting benefit—a mailing list of arthritis sufferers.

The ten-minute video from SmithKline Beecham is a model of commercial restraint. The video does not suggest that the viewer take Relafen for arthritis, only that he or she work with a doctor to manage arthritis instead of simply living with the condition. The attractive arthritic stars of the film include a man in his 70s riding a mountain bike and a fitness-walking woman in her 40s. They present a vision of the kind of active life that any arthritis sufferer would appreciate, and this positive message is linked to the product only by implication.

Relafen and other Nonsteroidal Anti-Inflammatory Drugs (NSAIDs) have broadened treatment options for people with arthritis, even though the side effects can be severe for some users. Up to one in four users has minor gastrointestinal side effects such as heartburn. One in six has "significant" side effects, and 1 to 2 percent have such severe problems they may need surgery. These severe problems can include major hemorrhage or perforation of the intestine, says Dr. David Y. Graham, a gastroenterologist and professor at Baylor College of Medicine in Houston.

"If you told a person who is buying a new car that they have a 2 percent chance of having a major accident...they would think about it," says Graham.

The difficulties linked to NSAIDs help open the market to new arthritis drugs and alternatives. In 1994, there were 18 such drugs in clinical trials. Also, 18 percent of U.S. adults used an unconventional therapy to treat arthritis during a 12-month period in 1990, according to a study published in 1993 in *The New England Journal of Medicine*. Another 7 percent saw an unconventional health provider such as a chiropractor or an acupuncturist for treatment of arthritis.

Alternative therapies and new drugs should continue to gain ground among women with arthritis as baby boomers, who favor alternative medicine, reach their prime years for arthritis. The most common form of the disease, osteoarthritis, usually strikes after age 50.

The Boom Years

As baby boomers develop arthritis, their demands can be expected to change the way manufacturers and health providers serve people with the problem. Baby boomers will not passively accept their physical limitations, says Hargis. "As this group ages, health concerns will be a major issue. Arthritis will affect about one in five people. The previous generation has said, 'These are things you have to live with.' Baby boomers won't accept that. They'll say, 'What exercise should I do? What medicine?'"

Foundation officials hope baby boomers will use some of that initiative to push for more research. "Right now Americans spend more on unproven remedies, like copper bracelets, than on trying to cure the disease," says Hargis.

They also hope that the coming surge in arthritis sufferers will result in demands that managed-care plans allow people with arthritis to be treated by arthritis specialists. "In this era of managed care and gatekeepers, most of the gatekeepers have little experience with arthritis. We have to educate the gatekeepers," says Dr. Doyt Conn, senior vice president for medical affairs for the Arthritis Foundation.

Women with arthritis offer a substantial opportunity for marketers who know their customers. Vigorous competition in the arthritis marketplace will make success more difficult, as baby boomers with arthritis will be more willing to seek new and alternative therapies. Claims about the effectiveness of a drug or therapy will be challenged vigorously by a new, more discriminating generation of arthritis patients. Successful products and services will target the oldest old and the youngest old with realistic promises for an independent life.

Incontinent But Active

It was the best of ads, it was the worst of ads. That was the verdict from older adults when market researcher Margaret Wylde asked them about advertisements for Depends incontinence products. Twenty-two percent of those surveyed said it was the best ad they saw directed to seniors. Another 19 percent said it was the worst.

The ambivalence among older adults about Depends advertisements is only one of the challenges for marketers in this competitive category. Most of the people Wylde surveyed liked actress June Allyson, the spokeswoman for the product, but many found the topic distasteful. "People don't like laxative ads or incontinence ads," says Wylde. "They don't like negative ads."

In the two decades since incontinence products were introduced, marketers have broken several barriers of silence about the topic. Their efforts have changed people's lives, says Cheryle B. Gartley, president of the Simon Foundation for Continence in Wilmette, Illinois. "We would get a lot of calls saying, 'I'm not the only one! Kimberly Clark wouldn't advertise just for me.'"

Incontinence remains difficult for many people to discuss. The Simon Foundation, founded in 1983, runs ads that say "Sshhhhh! Millions of Americans have a problem too embarrassing to talk about. Until now."

About 13 million Americans suffer from incontinence, and more will acquire the problem as the population ages. "There are a lot of myths about incontinence. One is that it is caused by aging," says Gartley, who suffers from incontinence in her mid-40s. "It is nondiscriminating, affecting all socioeconomic groups, races, and ages."

Still, the problem is most common among older women. Statistics about incontinence are sketchy, in part because so many people fail to seek help. But studies indicate that incontinence is twice as common in women over age 60 than it is among men the same age. It is estimated to affect between 15 and 35 percent of people aged 60 and older, according to the foundation. The problem affects between 1.5 and 5 percent of men and between 10 and 30 percent of women aged 15 to 64, in that age group, according to a survey by the United States Department of Health and Human Services Public Health Service. Demand for help with incontinence should increase as the number of better-educated women in their 60s increases.

Supermarket sales of incontinence products already are showing dra-

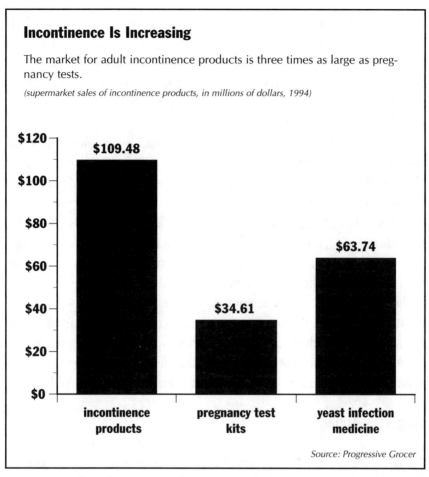

Incontinence Is Increasing

The market for adult incontinence products is three times as large as pregnancy tests.

(supermarket sales of incontinence products, in millions of dollars, 1994)

Source: *Progressive Grocer*

matic growth. Sales increased 18 percent between 1993 and 1994 and another 17 percent between 1994 and 1995, according to a report from *Progressive Grocer* magazine. In 1994, supermarkets sold $109.5 million in incontinence products, far more than supermarket sales of condoms ($39.5 million), douches ($65.5 million), and pregnancy tests ($34.6 million).

Before incontinence products were marketed to the general public, incontinent women typically used menstrual protection products, says Nancy Loos, an industry information analyst for H.P. Hamacher and Associates in Milwaukee, Wisconsin. In addition to the 50 percent of the people who buy incontinence products for themselves, about one-half of nursing home residents are incontinent and require the products.

The new openness about incontinence could actually limit sales of the products in the future. As women learn more about how common incontinence is, they may be more willing to seek medical help that could eliminate the problem.

"Until recently, doctors often said, 'You've had five babies, you're 80, you'll have to live with it'," says Carol Brink, a resistered nurse and associate professor at the University of Rochester School of Nursing. "Health providers didn't know what to do."

The picture has changed over the past few decades. Effective therapies include exercise, changes in lifestyle, medicine, and surgery. Women with incontinence now are advised to seek help quickly, because those who wait are less likely to be treated effectively, says Brink.

The success of incontinence products belies stereotypes about squeamish older women. While mature women may not enjoy hearing about incontinence products, their purchases have driven the success of Depends, Attends, and other products like them, offering hope for marketers of other products that address embarrassing health problems.

Long-Term Living

For decades, nursing homes have been seen as options of last resort. In 1993, the average American was more frightened by the prospect of putting a parent in a nursing home than by the idea of a parent dying suddenly, according to a poll conducted for *Health* magazine. Yet at the same time, nursing homes easily filled their beds without having to spend much on marketing.

In recent years, the picture has changed dramatically. There's no evidence that the image of nursing homes has changed, or that demand for them has dropped. But marketing has assumed new importance. "Long-term care never had to market itself before," says Francine Patella Ryan, marketing manager for the Jewish Home in Brighton, New York. "Now, marketing is a matter of survival."

Nursing homes continue to have occupancy rates of 90 percent or higher. Between 1980 and 1990, the number of Americans in nursing-home beds increased 24 percent, to 1.8 million people, according to the Census Bureau. But the need to boost revenue or profits makes marketing essential. One key element is to maintain the right "mix" of patients, including some private-pay patients. At the Jewish Home, 85 percent of patients have their costs covered by Medicaid, the federal health-insurance program for the poor. Medicaid pays less than private-pay patients for the same services.

New nursing-home services are being marketed vigorously to private-pay patients. These include day care for older people, which is often based at a nursing home; assisted-living facilities; and facilities that offer temporary services for people recuperating from broken bones or other problems. They also include facilities that combine nursing homes with other types of accommodations for more independent older people. As the industry tries to attract older people who could remain at home, marketing will be more important than ever.

Women are 72 percent of nursing-home residents, and they are also a majority of home-care patients. An increasingly well-educated, financially independent, demanding female health consumer will expect more information, more options, and more respect for diversity than the current generation of older women do.

Shape of the Market

Predicting the future market for long-term-care services is risky. Current rates of use do not account for factors such as extended life expectancy, new technology that makes the disabled elderly more independent, or new types of long-term care. For example, nursing homes of the future could provide services for older people in their own apartments using modems and telemetry, a practice that uses electrical equipment to collect and process data from one location and send it to another.

But regardless of the changes, it is clear that demand for some types of long-term care will grow as the population of older Americans increases. Nursing-home expert Joshua Weiner predicts the population in nursing homes will increase from 2.2 million in 1993 to 3.6 million by 2018. Weiner, a research associate for The Urban Institute, predicts there could be nearly 9 million people in nursing homes by 2050. His predictions are based on the total number of elderly people who enter and leave nursing homes in a given year. This number varies because many old people are seriously ill and die soon after entering a nursing home.

Census Bureau data suggest similar increases. If current rates of population growth continue, that would mean 3.1 million residents by 2000, 4.4 million by 2020, and 8.2 million by 2050.

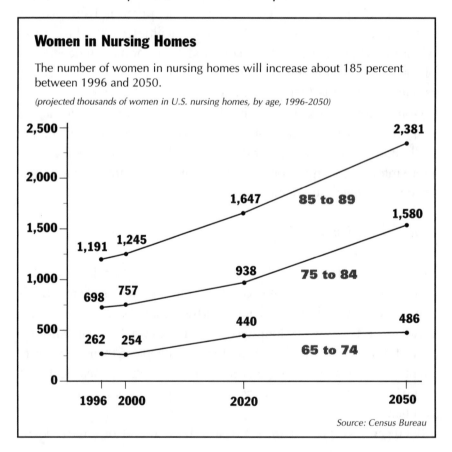

Women in Nursing Homes

The number of women in nursing homes will increase about 185 percent between 1996 and 2050.

(projected thousands of women in U.S. nursing homes, by age, 1996-2050)

Source: Census Bureau

Growth in the number of women in nursing homes should be more dramatic. Census data suggest that the number of 65-to-74-year-old women living in nursing homes should increase 60 percent between 1996 and 2020, and the number of 85-to-89-year-old women in nursing homes should increase 32 percent in that period if current rates of nursing-home residence continue. The oldest old have special needs. They require more attention than the typical nursing-home patient of the past, notes Ryan of The Jewish Home. "They're living longer, but they are more frail," she says.

Home-care services have already seen dramatic increases. The market for home care grew at an annual rate of about 10 percent between 1986 and 1991, and an estimated 12 percent annually between 1991 and 1996, according to Find/SVP and the National Association for Home Care. Total spending on home care has grown from $11.6 billion in 1987 to $26.5 billion in 1995, according to the association.

Home-care users usually do not receive around-the-clock care, which is often less expensive if provided in a nursing home. They include everyone from women with arthritis in need of a daily visit to women dying of cancer. Marilu Pittman, deputy director of marketing for the association, says she and other baby boomers like her should guarantee substantial growth in demand for home care. "Unless all of us in my age bracket just drop dead, I don't see how it can do anything but grow."

Sending the Message

An older woman works happily in the computer lab. Another woman sits absorbed in her reading, surrounded by books and plush rugs. The marketing for Kendal at Ithaca (New York) reflects the well-educated target audience for the community that opened in 1995 near Cornell University. "The library reflects the extraordinary population of Kendal," the ad copy says. "I don't think you'd find another place on earth with such a collection of interesting people." While Kendal at Ithaca just opened, the Kendal community in Hanover, New Hampshire has a waiting list that takes up to a decade for some types of housing.

For years, senior living communities portrayed the active life when selling independent housing. Nursing homes had nothing to do with such promotion. But facilities such as Kendal, which offer everything from independent to assisted living and a nursing home, must market differently. They depend on older people who could live elsewhere, but choose assisted living for its convenience, security, and companionship. Residents pay an entry fee and a monthly fee that covers housing, food, recreation, and most medical costs, including possible nursing-home care.

Promotional material includes everything from photos of residents cross-country skiing to explanations of the financial security in having health needs covered. "Wouldn't you like to be able to predict the bulk of your costs of living for the remainder of your life?" a brochure asks. Such appeals to financial security are particularly attractive to women, who are more likely in their older years to be poor and less likely to be confident about earning income through investments.

The marketing of the Summit, another continuing-care community being constructed by the Jewish Home in Brighton, New York, also emphasizes financial security. "Life Care: It's Almost Too Good to Be True!" the brochure announces. The direct-mail brochure shows Annette Osband, a volunteer at the Jewish Home, who exults that her bridge game should be able to keep running once she moves in because so many of her friends are considering the same move. Her concerns as a widow are shared by millions of other American older women: "There will come a time when I won't want the responsibility of leaky roofs, lawn care, and the like."

The Jewish Home appeals to older people with other options. The short-term rehabilitation center at the home is marketed through newspaper advertisements and direct mail as a place where people with temporary problems, such as recovery from hip-replacement surgery, can recuperate. Short-term care is generally paid for by health insurers, which offers the Home another source of income.

The Home also markets its adult day-care center in newspaper advertisements. Such centers are growing faster than any other type of long-term care, says Dr. Burton V. Reifler, a professor of psychiatry and behavioral medicine at Wake Forest University in Winston-Salem, North Carolina. The number of centers has grown from less than 100 to over 3,000 in the last two decades.

Adult day-care centers are an acceptable compromise to many older people who otherwise might move to a nursing home. "Day care offers a frail elderly person the chance to go somewhere in the morning and return home at night," says Reifler. "It's more like a normal life." Day care also appeals to dual-career couples who do not have a spare adult to care for an older parent during work hours.

Many nursing homes focus their marketing on the discharge planners of local hospitals. Staff members of Alamo Heights Health and Rehabilitation Center in San Antonio visit discharge planners at least five or six times a week, says spokeswoman Cynthia Miller.

Other homes open their facilities to the community as part of a marketing strategy. The 21 facilities owned by the for-profit Athena Healthcare Systems offer a variety of community services for free, says Tim Brown, marketing specialist for the Southington, Connecticut-based company. Support groups and community organizations meet free of charge in Athena nursing homes, and the homes offer free blood-pressure screenings to the community. The strategy is to impress potential residents with the cleanliness, appearance, and friendliness of a facility before they need it.

Programs like these make sense, because a person's personal experience and friends are critical to their choice of nursing homes. Word of mouth is the primary source of private-pay patients, according to a 1992 survey of 272 nursing-home administrators. Discharge planners at hospitals are the second major source of such patients, and physicians are third.

Marketers of nursing homes still depend heavily on conventional marketing. Three-quarters of them use ads in the yellow pages, two-thirds buy newspaper ads, and 63 percent use direct-mail brochures, according to the 1993 edition of the *Marion Merrell Dow Managed Care Digest*.

Providers of long-term home health care usually do not sell their services directly to consumers. This is largely because of the complicated regulations surrounding home care and its coverage by Medicare, Medicaid, and insurers.

"You can buy it for yourself," says Marilu Pittman of the National Association for Home Care. But few people can afford to pay for home care themselves. Only 3 percent of home-health-care services were paid for out-of-pocket in 1992. Of all home-care services, 31 percent were paid for out-of-pocket. Most home-care agencies target physicians and discharge planners, who know the rules and refer patients to care providers.

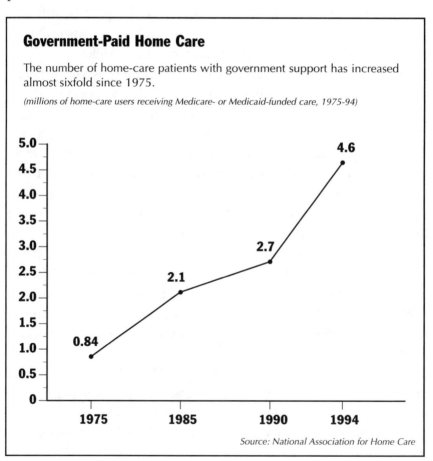

Government-Paid Home Care

The number of home-care patients with government support has increased almost sixfold since 1975.

(millions of home-care users receiving Medicare- or Medicaid-funded care, 1975-94)

Source: National Association for Home Care

Home-care marketers have an opportunity to promote their reputation and reliability to the public, because a growing number of families will need their services. Eight out of ten informal home-care givers are unpaid, the home-care organization reports. Three out of four of these informal caregivers are women, according to the group. As greater numbers of women enter the workplace, informal caregiving should become more difficult to provide. This dilemma will increase public demand for new solutions, creating new opportunities for marketers.

Future Plans

Just as day care for children has become commonplace, adult day care should become an increasingly popular form of long-term care as women remain in the workplace. Reifler predicts that there is room for three times the number of adult care centers in the future.

"Nursing homes still play a vital and important role," say Reifler, who is project director for Partners in Caregiving, a Robert Wood Johnson Foundation national program involving adult day care.

Yet adult day care is already adapting to fill the need of dual-income couples with a parent at home. Many of the centers have expanded their hours to serve working people, and many offer transportation and bathing services.

Assisted living should also change the market. Though assisted living is currently not covered by most insurers, it may be covered in the future if it emerges as a less expensive alternative to nursing homes. Women who want to remain independent without mowing the lawn or cooking their own meals may find assisted living ideal.

To attract new residents to long-term care, marketers may need to update their views. Changing social standards include greater public acceptance of lesbians and gay men, increasing rates of divorce, and higher numbers of never-married women. These will combine to change the picture of aging women in the future.

Long-term-care facilities would do well to be sensitive to lesbians, says Marcia Freedman, director of marketing and public relations for the

American Society on Aging. Freedman has worked with a group of Baptist nursing homes on the issue. "Market research studies are showing gay men and lesbians are anywhere from 2 to 10 percent of the population," she says.

Freedman says that many simple measures can be taken to make facilities for the aged appeal to lesbians. These may include training staffers to be sensitive to alternative lifestyles, offering equal-opportunity statements that include sexual orientation, and changing intake forms so they have more options than the conventional choices of single, married, divorced, or widowed.

Other segments that have been overlooked include Hispanic Americans, who are especially apprehensive about sending older relatives to nursing homes. As the number of Hispanic Americans increases, there will be a greater need for long-term care for older Hispanics. Nursing homes and other facilities with Spanish-speaking aides and physicians will have an edge.

Nontraditional services for older women should also have a bright future. Home care can serve only a fraction of mature women and men in need. Those who do not have serious health problems but who need some household help often have difficulty finding reasonably priced services.

Basic household assistance can keep older people out of nursing homes and make their independent lives last longer. But few businesses offer such services to older people, says Richard A. Lee, who worked as a consultant for a Minneapolis home assistance program. Lee helped develop a registry of state-approved businesses that serve seniors.

Long Lives

Over the past few decades, doctors have developed a dazzling array of surgical procedures and drugs that can prolong life. For some Americans, these efforts result in lives that are prolonged without hope in hospitals and nursing homes. But most Americans can look forward to an old age that is not dominated by infirmity or pain.

Health marketing to mature women must go beyond the old stereotypes of shy, sedentary crones, and move ahead to more realistic concerns. Aggressive efforts to find out what older women want could yield a large return.

The oldest old are a shifting target, as demographic changes will make them more discriminating. When a new generation of professional women reaches old age in the 21st century, they will question products and services more vigorously and demand more detailed answers about product safety and effectiveness.

Older women will probably become more affluent in the coming years, so expensive personal products could have a larger market than they did in the past. This could include everything from comfort items for women suffering from arthritis to hospital programs offering spa-like services to women following treatment for breast cancer.

Products and services that offer mature women independence, knowledge about how to manage their health problems, and the power to remain active in spite of their problems will become increasingly lucrative. As they struggle with the problems of aging, older women are a market that can only become stronger and more affluent.

Chapter 7

Women's Health Centers: Defining What Works

T he patients wear roomy gowns that cover their entire bodies. A masseuse's office is down the hall from the internist. The universally despised weigh-in ritual of patients has been banished. "We've done a lot of work on what women really want in health care." "We don't weigh women unless it is essential," says Maxine Brinkman, developer of the women's center at North Iowa Mercy Health Center in Mason City, Iowa.

For the past three decades, women's health centers have been offering women alternatives to regular medical care. The field began as part of the women's movement in the 1960s. Since then it has evolved, expanded, and diversified. Some women's health centers are primary-care centers linked to big hospitals; others are independent, not-for-profit centers specializing in maternity or breast care. In 1993, there were approximately 3,600 women's health centers in the U.S., according to a survey conducted by Carol S. Weisman, Ph.D., Barbara Curbow, Ph.D., and Amal J. Khoury, Ph.D., of Johns Hopkins University.

Mainstream health marketers may struggle to understand what women want. But women's health centers have been defining what women want for years. At the same time, women's health centers are struggling to survive the economic challenges in health care that have closed hundreds of hospitals. Between 1985 and 1995, many women's centers closed and others merged with larger organizations to remain open. In 1996, almost all of them are learning how to succeed in the demanding world of managed care.

As the push to save money continues, women's health centers must shape their services to satisfy women while they also satisfy health insurers and corporate financial officers. Successful programs are finding ways to combine innovative services and an appealing environment with cost-effectiveness.

The successes and failures of women's health centers are a blueprint of what works and what doesn't work in marketing health care to women. A warm and welcoming environment is nice, but it is not enough to keep women as patients. "What keeps them here is expertise and empowering women," says Brinkman. "We're treating the patients the way we ourselves would like to be treated."

A Separate Place

Health centers specifically for women are nothing new. Women's hospitals first appeared in the U.S. in the early 1800s, and family-planning clinics emerged in the 1920s. But the use of the term "women's health center" began in the 1960s, when feminists drew back from organized health care to launch freestanding clinics of their own. Early women's health centers, such as the Feminist Women's Health Centers launched in Los Angeles in 1971, gave women advice about how to conduct their own gynecological examinations, as well as providing contraceptive and abortion services. Some also offered primary health care.

By the middle 1970s, freestanding childbirth centers emerged to provide natural childbirth using midwives. A second wave of hospital-affiliated women's health centers opened in the 1980s to serve the many baby-boom women seeking personalized health care. By 1994, almost one in four acute care hospitals had women's health centers, according to the American Hospitals Association. Breast health centers also emerged in the 1980s, as concern about breast cancer climbed among American women.

Virtually any practice can define itself as a women's health center, so there is a huge variation in the quality, size, and purpose of the centers.

Some women's health centers in the 1990s are successful and well-established; others offer little besides a name and a marketing plan. "Sometimes all they are is a closet," says Karl Bartscht, chief executive officer of the health consultants Chai Systems in Ann Arbor, Michigan.

Even in the turbulent 1990s, new centers continue to open. The first for-profit Spence Center for Women's Health opened in Cambridge, Massachusetts in 1995, and a second opened in suburban Boston in 1996. The practice offers a combination of traditional medical services, such as primary-care physicians and podiatrists; screening services, such as mammography and ultrasound; and nontraditional therapies, such as acupuncture and muscle therapy. The Cambridge office, which

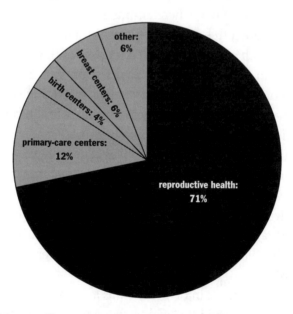

The World of Women's Health

Almost three-quarters of the estimated 3,600 women's health centers in the U.S. are focused on birth and reproduction.

(share of women's health centers by type of services offered, 1993)

other: 6%

breast centers: 6%

birth centers: 4%

primary-care centers: 12%

reproductive health: 71%

Note: Total does not add to 100 due to rounding.   *Source: Jacobs Institute of Women's Health*

had 8,000 to 9,000 patient visits during its first year, is the first of what owners hope will be a 40-center business.

Centers such as Planned Parenthood, which offer services and information about contraceptives, make up the bulk of women's health centers. About seven in ten women's centers in 1993 considered themselves primarily reproductive health centers, according to Weisman et al.'s Women's Health Center Survey. Another 12 percent were primary-care centers, 6 percent were breast centers, 4 percent described themselves as birth centers, and 6 percent were other centers. The centers served about 14 percent of all women aged 15 and older in 1993, for a total of 14.5 million women.

As the population ages, breast-care centers will see greater demand for their services. A total of 83 percent of women served by breast-care centers were aged 40 and older in 1993, according to Weisman et al.'s survey.

Primary-care centers attract an even mix of older and younger women today, but many of them may shift to a greater focus on mid-life and older women in the next decade. Primary-care centers for women

Who Uses Women's Health Centers?

Breast-care centers are well-positioned for an aging population of women.

(percent of patients at types of women's health centers, by age, 1993)

	primary care	reproductive health	birth	breast	other
	n=107	n=106	n=69	n=102	n=83
under 18	7%	15%	10%	0%	6%
18 to 29	43	55	46	5	22
30 to 39	16	18	32	12	21
40 to 49	14	7	8	26	21
50 to 64	13	3	2	34	17
65 and older	8	1	1	23	11

Note: Data are self-reported averages from the 467 centers in study.
Source: Jacobs Institute of Women's Health

also can expect to gain more patients as health care shifts its focus to primary-care providers. "Primary care is where the growth is going to be," says Weisman, a professor in the Department of Health Policy and Management in the School of Hygiene and Public Health at Johns Hopkins University.

Meanwhile, birth centers and reproductive health centers will face limited population growth among their primary target of childbearing women. Reproductive-health centers attract the youngest women, with 70 percent of patients under age 30. Birth centers attracted a slightly older client, with 78 percent in the prime childbearing years of 18 to 39. Marketing such services effectively will become more important between 1995 and 2005. The population aged 25 to 35 should decline, and the number of 15-to-24-year-olds will increase slightly.

Women's health centers succeed by promoting their different approach to care. The Maternity Center Associates, a birthing center owned by certified nurse midwives in Bethesda, Maryland, offers a class

---

Special Services

Most women's health centers offer education, exercise, and outreach programs.

(percent of women's health centers offering special services, by type of service, 1993)

	primary care n=107	reproductive health n=106	birth n=69	breast n=102	other n=83
open evening or weekend hours	49%	75%	86%	58%	67%
health hotline	50	58	46	66	76
support groups	62	39	65	64	80
exercise or diet class	52	16	59	33	71
translator/interpreter	44	70	54	53	58
speakers' bureau	60	68	74	78	81

Source: Jacobs Institute of Women's Health

called "The Motherhood Experience" that explains childbirth and the differences between midwives and physicians. Up to 90 percent of the women who attend the class choose to give birth at the center, says Marion McCartney, a nurse midwife who is a partner in the practice.

Women's health centers offer seminars on health problems like osteoporosis, and support groups linked to women's diseases such as endometriosis. They also offer a wide range of programs that sometimes stretch the conventional boundaries of health care. These include programs such as "Know When It's Time to Make a Change," a one-session course offering tips about how to move forward in life that is offered by the Women's Center of Christ Hospital and Medical Center in Tinley Park, Illinois. "The Internet—From a Woman's Perspective" is offered by Women's Health Care Plus center in Guilderland, New York.

This expansive definition of women's health is no coincidence. Women's centers that form relationships with women before they get sick have a better chance of attracting the same women as patients. Even in markets where managed care is not a factor, women's centers benefit from being perceived as a neighborhood center.

More than three-quarters of women's health centers use public programs or free screening events to market their services, according to the Weisman et al. survey. Almost as many run advertisements for their services. Other innovations that have worked around the country include:

- *Many types of care in one place.* Most women want to simplify their busy lives, so women's centers that offer a wide range of services are time-savers as well as life-savers. Women visiting the North Iowa Mercy Health Center can see their family doctor, talk to a social worker, and get a massage when it's all over. "Women's lives are complicated, so less running around is going to make a big difference," says Susan Reverby, a historian of women's health at Wellesley College.

- *Reduced waiting time.* Short waiting times are a powerful attraction for busy women. "When a woman has an appointment at one o'clock, they have an appointment with us at one o'clock," says Tillie Vastine, of the Women's Health Center of Allentown, Pennsylvania. Vastine's center is primarily for diagnostic visits, and they employ their own radiologists. As a result, "the patients' schedules and our technologists' schedules are never interrupted by a doctor," she says.

Other centers try to avoid the common practice of overbooking patients. At the Women's Health Center of Christ Hospital and Medical Center, women get coupons for a massage or other services if they have to wait a long time.

- *Nontraditional hours.* Evening and weekend appointments appeal strongly to working women and young mothers. The Women's Health Center at EHS Christ Hospital is open four nights a week and two Saturdays every month. "These are the hours that go the fastest," says manager Terry Mullady Guymon. The Weisman et al. study found that evening or weekend hours are offered at 86 percent of birth centers, 75 percent of reproductive centers, and 58 percent of breast centers.

- *Education as a top priority.* Women's enthusiasm for information is the essence of many women's health centers. The Maternity Center Associates in Bethesda teaches women to chart their own pregnancies, for example. "Women write in their own charts. They're taught how to weigh themselves," says Marion McCartney. "Women walk around reading their own charts. That's a strong message. This is your life."

Other practices offer more conventional educational resources, including support groups and patient libraries. The Mature Women's Health Center in Minneapolis offers patients videos and interactive computer stations. Planned Parenthood, with 900 health centers around the country, offers counseling and education to women. The organization's surveys show that women appreciate getting more than simply birth control. "They love the counseling,

---

Women's Work

Nationally, about one-quarter of obstetricians and gynecologists are women. That proportion is higher at most women's centers.

(proportion of women medical doctors and women medical or clinical directors at women's health centers, 1993)

	primary care	reproductive health	birth	breast	other
	n=107	n=106	n=69	n=102	n=83
women doctors......................	57%	33%	17%	24%	18%
women directors	64	35	50	35	35

Source: Jacobs Institute of Women's Health

---

something most providers don't do," says Wendy Lund, vice president of marketing.

- *Entry to a woman's world.* Many women's health centers promote their all-woman staff. The sense of being surrounded by women appeals to many women. "When they're here, it's low key," says McCartney of the Maternity Center Associates. "People are breastfeeding, they're in labor. I see them walking out with babies six hours old."

  Eighty-eight percent of the directors of women's health centers are women, and 93 percent of their nonphysician clinical staff are women, according to Weisman et al.'s survey. Women physicians are also more common at women's health centers than they are in general medical practice.

- *A comfortable, attractive environment.* A woman's center that looks great will not necessarily be successful. But appearance and comfort do make a difference to many women, according to Ruthie Dearing, a health marketer who has surveyed more than 40,000 women. Women appreciate everything from comfortable seating to free coffee, attractive wall decorations, and a telephone in the waiting room, she says.

"We always have flowering plants in the waiting room and fresh flowers," says Vastine of The Women's Health Center of Allentown. "Our artwork has been carefully selected. Whenever a woman is sitting or standing, there is art to reduce her tension." Still, quality care is most important. "There's hardly a woman who walks in here who does not mention the classical music, the soft tones, the cleanliness," says Vastine. "But I don't think she would come back for that. She would come back for efficiency, if she knows we're on time."

Proving Their Worth

Women's health centers, like their patients, have to juggle several roles without failing at any of them. High-quality medical care, educational programs, appealing decor, service, and flexibility are crucial, but they are not enough. Women's centers must also provide care that is cost effective.

Many women's centers close because they cannot prove their worth to the hospitals that own them, says Richard C. Ireland, president of The Snowmass Institute for Strategic Studies and publisher of *The Ireland Report on Women's Health Marketing* in Englewood, Colorado.

Directors of women's health centers are frequently unaware of the politics of their organizations, which gives them an inability to communicate with leading managers. Women's health directors "get too distant from the organization [that owns the center]," says Ireland. "Their political relationships are not that strong. Programs are cut because they never involved administrators."

Providing proof of worth isn't always easy for a women's health facility that stresses preventive medical care and long-term relationships. "At first, education was considered marketing," says Karen Schuss Rowinsky, of the women's health center at Stormont-Vail Regional Medical Center in Topeka. "It was a door to open the hospital." As time goes by, however, hospital officials want a more specific return on their investment. "One of the most difficult things is to track how many visits translate to hospital admissions," she says.

Tracking has to go beyond simply seeing if someone who visited once turns up as a patient. A visitor could have been referred to the hospital by a physician or by another source. Larger hospitals need to develop a marketing database to track such connections. Smaller community hospitals can partially substitute for a database by tracking specific indicators. Highland Hospital in Rochester, New York, was able to see that marketing women's programs resulted in an increased obstetrical case load, says vice president John Lee. Their tracking also showed that the programs raised awareness of the hospital and provided a public service. Further proof of effectiveness has eluded the hospital, says Lee. But the hospital expanded its women's center in 1996, even as it affiliated with another hospital.

Independent women's health centers face different challenges, including the need to work with managed care companies. In 1996, only 23 percent of HMOs had a contract or reimbursement agreement with a family-planning clinic or an abortion clinic, according to The Alan Guttmacher Institute of New York City. Sixty percent of these agreements are only for abortion. Family-planning clinics need to make aggressive efforts to market themselves to managed care systems.

Marketing was not stressed by most Planned Parenthood affiliates until recently. "Most of our patients in the past came in on referrals," says Lund, whose organization was founded by women's activists in 1916. "With managed care, we saw things change. Affiliates saw they had to start marketing."

Some Planned Parenthood centers now team up to negotiate with managed care groups. The centers can deliver larger numbers of patients and get a better deal in return. In other areas, Planned Parenthood uses the influence of board members to gain entrance into managed-care plans. Advertisements now encourage women to remain at Planned Parenthood beyond their early 20s, the age of the average patient. About 30 percent of women leave Planned Parenthood to seek other annual gynecological care, says Lund. Patient load increases as much as 10 percent after the ads run in some areas.

The organization is also launching other efforts to make its name more prominent. A 1996 book, *The Planned Parenthood Women's Health Encyclopedia,* is the first of a series to be published by Crown. The organization will take advantage of Crown's marketing to get more women into clinics, says Lund. It may also develop pregnancy tests, condoms, and other products that bear the Planned Parenthood name.

Understanding the Market

When Kathleen Lewton worked as a consultant to a hospital that was creating a women's health center, she discovered that local women's needs were completely different than what was anticipated by the hospital's medical staff. The medical staff helped Lewton and others draw up plans for the center. When they test-marketed them to women in the largely blue-collar community, the women rejected their plans. "They said, 'We won't go there,' remembers Lewton, author of *Public Relations in Health Care.* "We said, 'Would you visit a resource library?' They said, 'No. I want to get my kid into the doctor fast.' Women with kids generally didn't have time to be worried about their own health."

Once women's centers are established, patient surveys, community focus groups, and constant evaluation are essential. What works in Tampa will not necessarily work in Tulsa. Vastine says many programs have not worked in Allentown that work elsewhere. "We have tried to market counseling, but it doesn't fly. Is it the area we live in? In the Lehigh Valley, people may not want to part with money for that." Market research has not driven health-care decisions in the past, but women's health centers must find ways to attract women visitors to their centers.

Understanding women's statements about what they want is not always simple, says Guymon of the women's center at Christ Hospital and Medical Center. Women's voracious interest in health care can be a problem, for example. They may honestly report that they are interested in a topic, then bypass a program on the subject due to lack of time. "Everybody says to do focus groups and market research," says Guymon. "When you ask women what they want, though, it's difficult to define."

One of the worst programs Guymon presented was based on market research interviewing at malls. The women said they wanted to learn about premenstrual syndrome. Yet the program drew only three women. Research must be supplemented by experience and general knowledge of the market. After a decade at her women's center, Guymon says she has a sense of what will work and what won't.

The Future of Women's Health Centers

Managed care will continue to change the way women's health centers operate. Some freestanding centers have already chosen to affiliate with hospitals in order to obtain patients through managed care. More will follow. Ruth Shiers and her partner, Marion McCartney, decided to affiliate with St. Lukes Hospital in Bethlehem, Pennsylvania, in 1992, after operating an independent birthing center for 11 years. "As a little center, you just don't have the leverage to get into the market," says Shiers, who now operates an independent practice that is linked to the hospital.

Despite the link, Shiers' center continues to run advertisements that point out differences between its services and the services of conventional physicians practicing in the main birthing area of the hospital. "We market the high-touch, low-tech aspects of maternity care," says Shiers. "We spend a lot of time with people."

A women's health center can show its ability to provide efficient, cost-effective care in a number of ways. Some centers have a low rate of cesarean section deliveries. Others can point to success in early treatment of skin cancer. Programs for victims of domestic violence can also prove a women's center's worth to a hospital, says Ireland, if they keep women out of the hospital's emergency room.

The success of women's health centers has raised questions about their sex-specific focus. "The real risk group is men," says Sherrie Kaplan of the Primary Care Outcomes Research Institute of New England Medical Center. Men are more likely to die young and stay away from physician care when they are sick. "It would make sense to see the same women lobby for women's and men's centers, or family health-care centers."

A shift to family health care is already happening at some women's centers. The Women's Care Program at St. Joseph's Healthcare Systems in Albuquerque has some programs that are family-related or focused on men. The center offers programs encouraging women to bring their partners with them to hear about men's health, says Sally Piscotty, administrative director.

Another challenge for women's health centers lies in broadening their reach. Many centers serve primarily white, middle-class women, who are more likely than other groups to take good care of their health. This is most apparent at women's breast centers, where 75 percent of patients are white and only 9 percent receive Medicaid, according to the Weisman et al. survey. Reproductive health centers, birth centers, and primary-care centers all have larger percentages of minority women and Medicaid patients. Birth centers have the most low-income patients, with 35 percent of all patients covered by Medicaid.

As managed care becomes more dominant, all types of women's health centers will need to attract a broad range of women if they are to be truly effective in improving community health. But some women's centers may also need to change their very nature to survive. As the number of young women remains constant, demand for reproductive and birthing centers will probably not grow. Increasing numbers of centers may choose to switch their focus to mid-life or older women. About one-third of the 106 reproductive health centers Weisman et al. surveyed in 1994 were planning to focus more on mid-life or senior women over the next two years. About one-quarter of the centers intended to focus more on privately insured women in the future.

Women's health centers face many challenges, but advocates for the centers argue that they remain important. Women as a group still are sorely lacking in preventive-health services: 35 percent of American women did not have a pap smear in 1993, and 33 percent did not receive a clinical breast examination, according to the Commonwealth Survey on Women's Health. Thirteen percent of women did not get health care that was considered "needed" in 1993, compared with 9 percent of men, according to the survey. The numbers show that women still need special care directed to their needs.

Whatever the future of women's health centers, their success has already created an example for other medical practices and hospitals. "The good, comprehensive primary-care centers are definitely a model for what women want," says Weisman. Women want health care crafted to their schedule, their physical needs, and their desires for a healthy life. Women's health centers that can negotiate their way through managed care while meeting these standards should flourish.

Chapter 8

From Exercise to Echinacea: Marketing Prevention

It may not be the secret to eternal life or a guarantee of good health, but preventive medicine is the closest thing available. Exercise, healthy food, and regular screening tests, such as mammography and Pap smears, are essential parts of a healthy woman's life.

Yet American women resist the message. Only one in three strenuously exercises on a regular basis, millions are unconcerned about nutrition, and a sizable percentage of women never get screened for cancer. How do you successfully market products and services that promote health to women? "Everybody wants to know how to do this," says Mary O'Connell, director of prevention and nutrition for the American Cancer Society in Atlanta, Georgia.

Marketing prevention can be good business. Sales of NordicTrack exercise machines increased from $135 million in 1991 to $505 million in 1995. Sales of organic food and nutrition products increased 21 percent between 1993 and 1994, to $2.3 billion, according to *Natural Foods Merchandiser*. Yet persuading Americans to take care of themselves is tricky. "The information is out there," says Amy Carlson, a spokeswoman for NordicTrack in Chaska, Minnesota. "People know they should exercise. It's just providing them with the tools to do it."

Murky Swamps and Dirty Water

Doctors have always known that prevention is the cheapest and most effective way to remain healthy. Hippocrates suggested staying away from swamps where malaria was known to breed, and physicians in ancient Rome recommended that their patients use urine as a mouthwash to strengthen their gums. The emergence of modern research methods made prevention advice far more effective. In the 19th century, physician John Snow discovered that the well used for drinking water in a London neighborhood was elevating residents' risk of developing cholera. Londoners who drank clean water did not develop cholera.

Later research associated certain types of behavior with diseases. The link between lung cancer and cigarette smoking was documented in 1950, when researchers found that cigarette smoking was far more common in a group of 700 people with lung cancer than in a group of 700 people without the disease. Since then, researchers have used clinical trials and laboratory findings to prove that exercise helps strengthen the heart and reduce the risk of osteoporosis; that a good diet cuts the risk of certain types of cancer and heart disease; and that eating less salt helps to keep blood pressure down and reduces the risk of stroke.

These findings have been widely publicized. Stories on breast and ovarian cancer could be found in almost every magazine offering regular health coverage in 1995. Stories about nutrition were also common, according to Michael L. Laughlin, who examined magazine coverage in the November-December 1995 *Ireland Report on Women's Health Marketing*. One result is that many women already know what a healthy lifestyle requires. Forty percent of women believe that a good diet is the most important factor in staying healthy, according to a 1994 study conducted for the Center for Women Policy Studies. Thirteen percent say seeing a doctor regularly is the most important factor, and 12 percent say that exercise is the primary factor in good health. Another study, conducted by EDK Associates for *Redbook* magazine in 1992, found that 89 percent of women believe that diet can prevent ailments.

Relatively few women act on their knowledge, however. In order to stay healthy, 28 percent of women say they keep a good diet and 25 percent exercise regularly, according to the 1994 study by the Women's Center for Policy Studies.

The Great Divide

In the last decade, Americans have demonstrated a split personality toward preventive health care. In many ways, women do far less than they once did to stay healthy.

Sixty-eight percent of American women and men were overweight in 1995, compared with 58 percent in 1983, according to the Prevention Index. This may be due in part to the aging of the population, because it is normal to gain weight with age. Yet it still reflects a retreat from health. Women who gain 18 to 25 pounds have a 60 percent greater risk of a heart attack, according to a 14-year study of about 116,000 women.

Though the importance of nutrition in good health has been underscored by numerous studies, Americans were less likely to care about their nutrition in 1994 than in 1983. Specifically, Americans were less likely in 1995 to care about getting enough vitamins or minerals, eating enough fiber, eating less salt, or eating enough vegetables than they were in 1993, according to the Prevention Index. And 24 percent of women smoked in 1994, compared with 20 percent in 1993.

Yet there also are signs of an increased commitment to a healthy lifestyle. Sales of vitamins, minerals, herbs, and nutritional supplements have grown dramatically. From June 1994 to June 1995, sales of nutritional supplements increased 38 percent, according to ACNielsen. Sales of multiple vitamins increased 17 percent. Membership in health clubs increased from 16.5 million in 1992 to 19.2 million in 1995, according to the International Health, Racquet & Sports Club Association in Boston.

Testing for early detection of diseases has also become more common. The proportion of women aged 50 and older who received a mammogram and a clinical breast exam increased from 25 to 51 percent between 1987 and 1992, according to the National Center for Health Statistics.

The schizophrenic health habits of American women contain clues about what works and what does not work when marketing preventive health products and services. The most important rule is that there is no typical user of preventive health products and services. Women are less likely to exercise as they get older, for example, but they are more likely to take vitamins. NordicTrack's target audience is middle-aged men and women. Other exercise products, such as rollerblades, are marketed to younger people. Still, all successful marketing efforts for preventive health measures have some elements in common. Women are drawn to products and services that offer:

- *A positive image of health.* For years, health officials used fear to encourage the public to stay healthy. During World War I, posters of

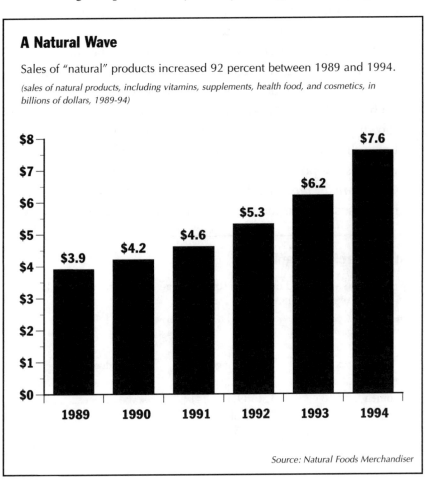

A Natural Wave

Sales of "natural" products increased 92 percent between 1989 and 1994.

(sales of natural products, including vitamins, supplements, health food, and cosmetics, in billions of dollars, 1989-94)

1989	1990	1991	1992	1993	1994
$3.9	$4.2	$4.6	$5.3	$6.2	$7.6

Source: Natural Foods Merchandiser

skeletons wearing evening gowns were used to scare the troops about syphilis. The posters did little to stop soldiers from having sex with infected women, however.

Fear might motivate some people, but it may actually discourage some others from getting screened for health problems. "If they have cancer, they don't want to find out," says Louise Galaska, deputy director of the Division of Cancer Prevention and Control at the Centers for Disease Control (CDC). "Fear doesn't work," adds Mary O'Connell of the American Cancer Society. "It paralyzes people. They don't take action." O'Connell says it is best to find positive reasons to seek screening, such as the promise of spending more years with children or grandchildren.

Fear also can paralyze women who are out of shape. Many women who are middle-aged or older did not exercise as girls. "They are terrified to come in here," says Betsy Larey of River Valley Athletic Club in Stillwater, Minnesota. A key to attracting older women is showing positive images of similar people in promotional material. Larey shies away from promotional photos of slim athletes: "We want to show people who are overweight and out of shape."

- *Child care for mothers.* River Valley provides everything from an indoor space maze and swings for preschoolers to a climbing wall

---

Who Exercises Regularly?

Men, young adults, and those with some college education are most likely to have an exercise routine.

(percent of U.S. adults who exercise strenuously three or more days per week, by sex, age, and educational attainment, 1996)

sex		age		education	
men	45%	18 to 29	50%	less than college	38%
women	34	30 to 49	41	some college	45
		50 and older	28	college grad	37

Source: Prevention Index

and supervised exercise machines for older children. "Parents can feel good about themselves because they know the kids are doing good things," says Larey, who also owns a club in Eau Claire, Wisconsin. The child-care program has a lot to do with River Valley's low turnover rate. It is 20 percent, while the industry average is between 35 and 40 percent, according to the International Health, Racquet & Sports Club Association. If parents believe their children are having fun, they are more likely to make exercise a regular part of their lives.

NordicTrack also attributes some of its success to women who are able to work out while their children are nearby. "You can watch the kids while you're working out," says Carlson. "It's convenient."

• *A reasonable price.* The most popular exercise activity among Americans is also one of the cheapest. In 1990, 45 percent of Americans walked for exercise, according to the National Center for Health Statistics. Gardening, the number-two activity, involved 26 percent of Americans. Calisthenics or general exercise was practiced by 18 percent of Americans. Price makes a difference, particularly among women who are likely to have less money to spend than men.

A Worsening Diet

America's eating habits have changed in the last decade, and most changes have been for the worse.

(percent of Americans who try to reach selected dietary goals, 1983, 1989, and 1995, and percentage point change, 1983-95)

Do you:	1983	1989	1995	change
try to eat enough fiber?	59%	60%	57%	-2
try to avoid eating too much fat?	55	58	52	-3
try to avoid eating too much sugar?	51	46	37	-14
try to get enough calcium?	50	55	50	0

Source: Prevention Index

Women may choose to sacrifice health screening if they cannot afford the price. In 1992, only 19 percent of uninsured women aged 50 to 64 received a mammogram, compared with 55 percent of women who had private insurance coverage. Free screenings will attract these underserved women.

· *Limited time commitment.* Herbal, nutritional, and vitamin supplement manufacturers promote their products as one of the quickest routes to good health. "The Next Best Thing to Eating Your Veggies," promises an ad in *Natural Foods Merchandiser* for Caro-Plete, a complex of alpha and beta carotenes from Carlson Laboratories in

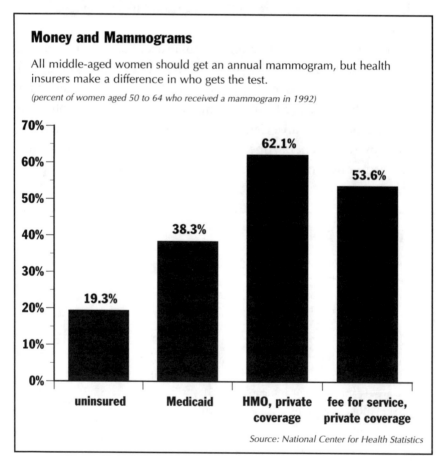

Money and Mammograms

All middle-aged women should get an annual mammogram, but health insurers make a difference in who gets the test.

(percent of women aged 50 to 64 who received a mammogram in 1992)

Source: National Center for Health Statistics

Arlington Heights, Illinois. Nothing could fit better into a busy lifestyle than a pill to replace the broccoli working women don't have time to cook.

Time is a factor in many women's purchases of a NordicTrack machine. By the time they leave work, go to a health club, change, and shower, working women may not get home until 7:30 p.m., says Carlson. With an exercise machine, "You can go home, throw on your sweats, and work out for 30 minutes. You can have dinner in the oven."

- *Low risk.* Women are drawn to preventive health products that offer them benefits without much risk. "A lot of people are concerned about the side effects of synthetic and chemical drugs," says Shane Herman, product manager for NaturaLife, a manufacturer of herbal, homeopathic, vitamin, and mineral products in Springville, Utah. "A good many of them make you drowsy or nauseated.."

  Many alternative supplements target conditions for which there is no medical "cure." Echinacea is one of the company's best-selling products, with national sales by NaturaLife and other manufacterers in the millions, according to *Newsweek.* "It keeps you from getting sick. If you do get sick, it keeps you from getting sicker," says Herman.

- *Proven benefits.* Perception can build a barrier to preventive health, or it can encourage a new level of care. One obstacle to older women receiving mammograms is a pervasive fatalism about cancer. "The expectation is that when you get older, you will get cancer," says O'Connell of the American Cancer Society. Older women sometimes feel they don't need a mammogram. The percentage of women having mammograms dwindles after age 60. In fact, mammograms are most effective in prolonging life for women aged 50 and older.

  Changing these attitudes is difficult. Women respond best to people with whom they are comfortable, says Galaska of the CDC.

Programs supported by the CDC include Witness, which uses women active in predominantly black local churches in Arkansas to promote breast health. Community workers such as these are the most credible type of health educators, she says.

One of the most effective public information campaigns was a massive effort mounted by the National Heart, Lung and Blood Institute in the 1970s to increase knowledge about cholesterol and high blood pressure. Most Americans in the 1990s know something about the connection between a healthy heart and having low cholesterol. The 1993 survey by EDK Associates found that 53 percent of women are more inclined to buy a product that advertises its low cholesterol content. One reflection of this knowledge is the fact that the death rate from stroke dropped 27 percent between 1982 and 1992. The success of the campaign stemmed from the ability of experts to offer a clear picture of risk and a manageable way to act on the problem.

- *Social appeal.* For members of the older women's workout class at River Valley Athletic Club, getting together after class is part of the routine. Group members, ranging in age from 55 to 83, often bring food to class and have a meal together. Social opportunities make women more likely to integrate exercise into their lives, says Larey, and such regularity is the key to staying fit. The appeal of walking among women may also stem from the social aspect of a regular walk with friends.

  Manufacturers of vitamins, herbal supplements, and organic food products have long depended on the social value of gathering shoppers together. In the 1960s, food cooperatives were formed across the country to purchase organic food and other alternative products. Today, food cooperatives still feature people working together with similar ideas about food and politics. The food cooperative in Brattleboro, Vermont, is one of the major social centers of the town, complete with a sit-down restaurant.

  Most working women don't have a lot of time to be sociable. But many will eagerly accept the chance to socialize if they can exercise or go food shopping at the same time.

Information for Health

As the population ages, more women will face a greater risk of health problems and a greater need for services and products that help them stay healthy. Many preventive medicine products have the greatest appeal among older people.

A walk through the extensive vitamin and supplement aisles of any Florida drugstore tells the story better than any survey. Statistics show that shoppers aged 50 and older spend more on liquid vitamin tonics and multi-vitamins than any other age group, according to ACNielsen.

Demographic and attitude changes among women will make a difference to marketers of preventive-health products. An increasingly well-educated market should make educational efforts more important. Women may retain their preference for solutions that are quick, cheap, and low-risk. More complex solutions will be successful if they show that they are worth the effort.

NordicTrack depends on an extensive educational marketing campaign to sell its exercise machines, which range in price from $299 to $2,000. Women are 45 percent of the company's customers. The company was a pioneer in promoting its equipment with lengthy "infomercials," packed with information about the benefits of exercise and NordicTrack. The company switched to print advertisements and shorter television spots in 1996, in part because previous ads already made the company name familiar to the public.

NordicTrack's marketing message to women, which runs in women's magazines such as *Self* and *Shape*, focuses primarily on weight loss. This is because 62 percent of women in 1991 said they watch their weight, according to EDK Associates. The men's message, marketed in magazines such as *Men's Health*, promotes the idea of using NordicTrack to build strength and overall health, along with weight loss.

Women who call NordicTrack's toll-free number are asked about the primary benefit they would like to achieve, with a list ranging from weight loss to strength to shaping and toning. They are then given information about particular products based on their answers. Such strategies have helped the company prove to women that NordicTrack is worth the money.

More-educated women will force marketers to offer more information about their products in the future. In 1996, criticism of the potentially lethal side effects of some herbal supplements reflected the limited government regulation of their content. Heightened scrutiny of supplements, vitamins, and herbal products can be expected in the future.

Marketers will need to tell consumers clearly what their products can and can't do. One leader in this area is General Nutrition Companies, a chain of health-food stores based in Pittsburgh. The company, which controlled 14 percent of the food supplement market in 1996, has opened prototype stores that offer shoppers information about the health claims of products. Customers enter information about a product into a computer, and discover whether there is strong evidence for health claims, questionable evidence, or unproved evidence. The company also trains its salespeople not to make wild promises about products. Such truthfulness gives customers the opportunity to buy unproven products without misleading them about the benefits.

Working for Health

As working women and working mothers continue to dominate the younger and mid-life markets, health marketers must offer products and messages that fit their lifestyle.

The American Cancer Society is launching a campaign to teach working women how to cook healthy foods and eat well when they get home from work. A key focus will be on how to manage the first 15 minutes after arriving home, the time when millions of working mothers and their children gobble up potato chips and pretzels. Such programs have the potential to help women through a difficult hour, when eating quickly is usually a bigger concern than eating nutritiously.

Programs should be geared to women who are pressed for time, says Kathleen Loughrey, former coordinator of nutrition and educational programs for the Office of Cancer Communications at the National Cancer Institute. "The interest and concern [about nutrition] is high," says Loughrey. "What has eroded is the availability of time. If people spend time planning a meal, they might plan something nutritious, instead of, 'I'm on my way to a meeting. What can I get to eat in the next three blocks?'"

Women need strategies to stay healthy, such as the idea of buying fruit they can grab on the way to work, or buying fruit in office cafeterias. Certain messages are more effective when encouraging women to eat well, says Loughrey. Her focus groups of women and men showed that the most motivating idea was having more energy.

To reach working women, health screenings must be available after work or on weekends. Workplace programs or articles in company newsletters about health screening, weight loss, ways to quit smoking, or other topics are all good ways to reach working women.

Some health centers even offer women career advice. The Women's Health Center of Christ Hospital in Tinley Park, and the Medical Center in Oak Lawn, Illinois, has a lunch group for businesswomen that focuses on ways to make them more competent as managers. While the program may not lead directly to mammograms, members are more likely to know what is available if they are regularly in contact with the administrator of the center, who routinely attends the program. "I am constantly asked health-related questions about women," says Terry Mullady Guymon, administrator of the Women's Health Center. Establishing contact with working women is the first essential step in showing them what they can do to be healthier.

The number of sedentary Americans remains high, but fitness should be of greater interest to midlife and older women in the future. In 1996, women in their 50s and older are much less likely than younger women to have played organized sports in school. But when baby-boom women who competed on their college lacrosse or basketball teams reach middle age, they will not want to stop being athletic. This market should drive interest in exercise and fitness programs for women. Older Americans already are exercising more. In 1992, 39 percent of older people were completely sedentary, compared with 43 percent in 1987, according to the CDC.

The appeal of quick, inexpensive, low-risk fixes to health problems is perennial. Marketers of health products that are quick and inexpensive will always have an edge. Marketers who sell health screening, or products that are more complicated and costly, must prove through education that what they provide is worth a woman's time and money. Outlandish claims will be a harder sell in the future, as better-educated women reach their mature years.

Health marketers selling disease prevention can only benefit from the flood of aging boomers reaching their 50s, because this is a turning point when risk of serious health problems climbs. But women will need proof that better health is attainable, and that it is worth making a sacrifice of time, money, or both.

Chapter 9
Moving Ahead

A middle-aged woman hikes briskly along a mountain lake shore. An older woman pulls a garden cart across an impossibly green summer lawn at the break of day. "Osteoporosis," the booklet from Merck reads. "The more you know, the better."

The look and sound of Merck's free booklet about osteoporosis makes it seem less like advertising for Merck's osteoporosis drug, Fosamax, and more like the bible of the women's health movement, *Our Bodies, Ourselves*. There is detailed information about the disease, sophisticated photography of healthy and unhealthy bone, and lucid descriptions of the potential risks linked to Fosamax. The women portrayed in the booklet are attractive but realistic looking, and utterly devoid of glamour.

Times have changed for health-care businesses that market to women. Gone are the days when women meekly took their medicine because it was recommended by a physician. Gone, too, are the days when drugs were advertised only to physicians because physicians were the only ones knowledgeable enough to understand drug information.

Medicine itself has changed. Hospitals and physicians once flourished as long as they provided good quality care, but today some of the best hospitals struggle to remain open. Doctors were once sole proprietors who were paid directly by their customers, but now they must compete for the attention of HMOs and other managed care providers. Alternative health providers, such as herbalists and acupuncturists, are increasingly popular. Women physicians are common in most markets.

Many physicians still see advertising as distasteful and choose not to overtly market their services. Yet the most effective health marketing draws directly from the traditional patient-physician relationship. Successful marketing of health care to women means providing health education and building trust while offering high-quality products or services.

American women in the 1990s want to know more about health care, but they are skeptical about the medical world. Women as a group are likely to become even more skeptical of marketing in the future, as savvy young adults move into their family years. "They have grown up with marketing in a way the rest of us have not," says Melissa Shepherd, who held focus groups of 18-to-25-year-old men and women for the National Center for HIV, STD and TB prevention at the Centers for Disease Control. "Young adults' radar for marketing strategies is fine-tuned," she says. "You have to be really careful about the messages."

Messages that appeal to one generation of women may seem false and offensive to others. It will be especially important to build loyal relationships with younger women and pay attention to their criticism of the way products are promoted. The criticism is unlikely to disappear as increasing numbers of well-educated women reach their mature years. Marketers will need to stay accountable about everything from the price of their products to the way they describe potential side effects.

Hospitals, physicians and other service providers must find ways to build new relationships with new patients and maintain their existing patients. Some providers will use sophisticated marketing techniques, such as database marketing, to gain a competitive edge. Others will develop new ways to publicize their services to women. A constant search for new ways to understand the women's market will be essential as women's wants and needs continue to change.

Information Industry

The power of computers will be central to health marketing in the future, as drug companies, product manufacturers, and hospitals find new ways to gather and use consumer databases. The potential of database marketing in women's health care is immense, given the billions of health dollars spent by women. Yet marketers must respect women's strong need for health information privacy, or the technique could do more harm than good.

Database marketing is a way for companies to acquire and use mountains of information about consumers. Kraft Foods uses information from more than 30 million customers who have filled out coupons and other information forms, for example. The company develops lists of people who use specific products, then sends them coupons and other special offers for the products they have purchased. By sending special offers only to Miracle Whip users, Kraft can get a better return on its marketing budget for that product.

Marketing mammograms is not the same thing as marketing mayonnaise. Yet database marketing is an effective tool for health marketers. Every gift pack mailed to a pregnant woman uses targeted mailing lists to encourage spending during the free-for-all of maternity spending. And every time The Methodist Healthcare System of San Antonio sends out information about menopause programs to the aging baby-boom women in its database, it too is taking advantage of this powerful technique.

Database marketing lets companies move beyond marketing to women based on demographic traits, such as their education level or age. Its power lies in the fact that people with similar demographics do not necessarily share the same need for health services, says Mary Kay Conlon, senior vice president of the Sachs Group in Evanston, Illinois, which specializes in database marketing for health firms. "Should you mail something about infertility to someone who has just had their fifth kid? I don't think so," she says.

Only about 20 percent of hospitals now use database marketing, says Conlon. Yet hospitals have a huge advantage over many other businesses because they already have extensive medical records on their patients. Once these record-keeping systems are computerized, this information can be sorted and used by marketers. It is not protected against such uses by law in 1996, although some lawmakers have proposed such a ban.

Database marketing gives hospitals the ability to custom-design newsletters, focusing on stories that particular consumers are most likely to read, says Conlon. Database marketing also allows hospitals to track precisely whether educational programs, women's health centers, or other programs are bringing new patients to the facility.

Yet health marketers who use database techniques must be careful to respect the private nature of many women's health conditions. Limitations placed on everything from contraceptive marketing to public discussions about incontinence make clear the continuing social awkwardness surrounding many women's health needs. Direct marketing that appeals to women suffering from incontinence to infertility is a risky move if women have not previously requested the information.

Most Americans are worried about invasions of their privacy. In fact, 47 percent are very concerned about threats to their personal privacy, and another 35 percent are somewhat concerned, according to the Equifax-Harris Mid-Decade Consumer Privacy Survey of 1995. Health marketers who use databases must be careful not to show consumers they know personal details if the consumer has not given them explicit permission to use the information in advance.

One way to raise the subject is to ask consumers when they provide information whether it may be used for marketing purposes. "If information is going to be used for purposes other than that for which it was collected, there should be notice," says Kathleen A. Frawley, director of the Washington, D.C. office of the American Health Information Management Association. "I would be concerned if I knew a hospital was going to use its database without notice to me or authorization." Frawley's group is working to make health records protected by law. "Your video rental records are protected and your consumer credit records are protected, but your medical records are not," she says.

Patients are not legally entitled to the knowledge that their records may be used for marketing. But marketing efforts to women that appear to take advantage of private information are unlikely to succeed if they make recipients feel violated. Hospitals and physicians have a lot to lose if they violate a patient's trust by abusing records. People who send in warranty cards or request information from a company usually understand that this information may be used for commercial purposes. This is not true about health records.

Health marketers must be meticulous in the way they use database marketing, and they must constantly be alert for potential problems. Obtaining consent to use patient information for marketing may be the smartest way to retain women as patients.

Many of the challenges facing health marketers are similar, such as navigating the new world of database marketing. But there are other issues unique to marketers in each category. Product marketers, for example, still face the age-old need to gain women's faith and trust.

Building Trust in Health Products

Critics have long accused health-product marketers of misleading the public. In the late 19th and early 20th centuries, for example, marketers' abuse of medical authority led to some of the earliest regulations on advertising. William Radam's "Microbe Killer," sold during the 1880s, was made up primarily of water and red wine.

Today's highly regulated pharmaceutical industry bears little resemblance to the patent medicine industry of the 19th century. Laws prohibit drug companies from publishing misleading or untrue information, and prescription products must be tested extensively before they are approved for sale. Yet critics continue to charge companies with overmarketing everything from Norplant birth-control to Fosamax osteoporosis medication. In 1993, journalists Donald Drake and Marian Uhlman reported that major pharmaceutical companies spend 20 cents of every revenue dollar on marketing and promotion, for a total of some $10 billion a year. Their book, *Making Medicine, Making Money*, painted a portrait of marketing run amuck at the expense of affordable health care.

Pharmaceutical companies use everything from free samples to test marketing and extensive advertising to boost sales. If sales are an indication, they are master marketers: industry leader Merck, for example, reported sales of $16.7 billion in 1995, an 11 percent increase from 1994. Yet increasing sales do not guarantee future success. Companies that lose their customers' trust will lose the business of the well-educated and critical women, the gatekeepers to most health care spending.

To succeed in the future, product marketers must follow several rules:

- *Be frank about side effects.* The greatest marketing disasters in women's health have involved products that promised too much. Physicians and the pharmaceutical companies that manufactured the drug DES claimed that it had no side effects and prevented miscarriages. These claims were ultimately proven false, but not before they caused great human suffering. The legacy of DES and other failed or misrepresented products is skepticism among women toward drugs and pharmaceutical companies. Marketing that fails to provide legible, comprehensible information about side effects could mean product failure when side effects occur. Product information should go beyond the requirements of the FDA, which allows health marketers to use print so small that it is difficult for older people to see, and daunting for many others to examine.

- *A human voice.* When Rogaine launched a hot-line for information about its hair-thinning product, women called with tales of woe about their life with hair loss. Pharmacia & Upjohn, Inc., staffed its hot-line with real people—not taped messages—and used the information gathered from callers to sharpen its picture of what women wanted from the product.

  In a world where people often see open discussion of health problems as tasteless, information lines can offer consumers support while they link prospective customers to a company. A good customer service line can humanize a big company and give callers information that is tailored to their needs. Toll-free information lines are particularly well-suited to working women who do not have the time to wait for a physician's call.

  Increasingly, product marketers are establishing trust by offering customers access to information through personal computers. Such strategies make good sense for working women who are hungry for health information and conversation, and for companies seeking a humane public image.

- *More direct-to-consumer advertisements.* Some health products should never use consumer advertising, particularly those for acute or life-threatening illnesses. But the old rule, "Doctor knows best" no longer applies in many health markets. Direct-to-consumer advertising suits women who want to be a partner with their physician in deciding which medicine is best.

- *Show them you care.* Drug companies in particular must work against the public perception that they are more concerned with money than health. They can do this by supporting good causes and publicizing their own good works. A statue at the Whitehouse Station, New Jersey, headquarters of Merck that shows a child leading a blind man was reproduced in the company's 1995 annual report to honor Merck's efforts to end river blindness, a preventable disease that is common in Africa and Latin America. The company estimates that product donations to support campaigns such as the river blindness effort totaled over $90 million in 1995.

Health-product marketers must focus on gaining women's trust. Providers of health services, such as hospitals and physicians, must move beyond old-fashioned notions of being above the marketplace in order to survive the managed care era.

In Sickness And In Health

Hospitals have marketed their services for years. Until recently, however, marketing was seen as unnecessary by many other providers of health care. "When I first arrived here, the staff people said, 'We don't do marketing. But we would like to,'" says Wendy Lund, vice president of marketing for Planned Parenthood Federation, who started her job in January 1994.

Many health organizations didn't need marketing until rapidly escalating health-care expenses made managed care and other cost-cutting strategies more attractive. As organizations such as Planned Parenthood Federation and physician groups explore the potential of marketing, they must walk a fine line between the old and new ways of doing business.

Hospitals, physicians, and other providers cannot become so marketing-oriented that they sell unnecessary services, or they will be vulnerable to the type of criticism health-product marketers have encountered. Indeed, many of the higher cost strategies used by drug companies pose a dilemma to doctors who need to cut costs. Yet physicians, hospitals, and other health providers have assets that health products do not. Marketing their services is easier in many ways than promoting a new health product.

American women still trust their physicians for health information. Women are more likely to receive health information very often or fairly often from their physicians than from any other source: 64 percent of women do so, compared with 55 percent of men, according to a 1995 poll from Roper Starch Worldwide. Friends and family are women's second most popular source of health information, with 60 percent of women often obtaining health news from them. About one out of five women says that advertisements are a source of health information very often or fairly often, while 57 percent say they use television often for health information.

Physicians and their hospitals are already trusted. They can market their services in ways that do not compromise this trust, if they follow these rules:

- *Offer education.* Women depend on their physicians for information, but physicians often are difficult to contact unless there is an emergency. Physicians, hospitals, and health insurers who offer

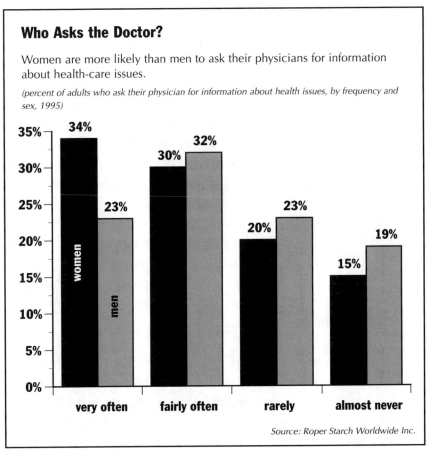

Who Asks the Doctor?

Women are more likely than men to ask their physicians for information about health-care issues.

(percent of adults who ask their physician for information about health issues, by frequency and sex, 1995)

very often: women 34%, men 23%
fairly often: women 30%, men 32%
rarely: women 20%, men 23%
almost never: women 15%, men 19%

Source: Roper Starch Worldwide Inc.

women more information will build greater loyalty and reduce unnecessary patient visits, which is a critical goal of managed care.

Some information lines offer pregnant women telephone access to a nurse 24 hours a day. The Bright Futures Program for pregnant women offered by United Healthcare Corporation of Minnetonka, Minnesota, is used by health plans and employer groups that belong to United Health Care programs.

Another information line is offered by pediatricians in Denver through the Children's Hospital. The phone line staffed by pediatric nurses is open to parents when their regular doctor's office is closed. In 1995, the program offered coverage for 97 percent of the individual practitioners in Denver, according to *Patient Care* magazine.

The service is a boon to working women who need answers to health questions outside conventional work hours.

Other approaches can be used by large or small physician practices. Resource libraries in physicians' offices or hospitals are often helpful. Group practices and hospital-based practices can also expand the use of health educators who are not physicians to provide information to patients about complicated topics such as estrogen therapy. Educators can also provide telephone information, which is particularly important for working women.

- *Adopt a working woman's schedule.* Women are a permanent addition to the work force, so hospitals and physicians can gain patient appreciation by altering their hours and cutting waiting times. Medical practices should examine their procedures for waiting times and be vigilant about explaining why patients must wait when there are emergencies.

- *Surround them with warmth and caring.* Women leave physicians who treat them poorly and are drawn to those who communicate well. Marketing to women will be more effective if it focuses on human elements, rather than the newest medical machinery. In other words, an advertisement that shows a physician's record of helping area women and Ethiopian refugees may carry more weight than an advertisement about her expertise operating a magnetic resonance imager.

- *Promote women-centered care.* As more women enter the medical profession, the marketing appeal of practices with women physicians will diminish because it will be so common. But men physicians will continue to outnumber women physicians for several decades, so the appeal of women-centered care will remain a powerful marketing tool.

Decision-Makers of the Future

The tools of medicine will continue to change. A century ago, there was no birth-control pill; indeed, the use of birth control was illegal in many states. There were no estrogen supplements and no sanitary napkins. The sexually transmitted disease syphilis often caused death, because there was no effective treatment.

We cannot know how health therapies will change in the next century. Fortunately, health marketers need not be concerned with the far distant future. Whatever the technological advances, women are still likely to be the most important household decision-makers when it comes to health care. "This rule of thumb hasn't changed over the last 25 years, when there have been so many other changes," says Judith Langer, president of Langer Associates, a market research and trend consulting firm in New York City. "I don't think it will in the future."

Women's health concerns will be increasingly visible as baby boomers age. The same generation that railed against menopause in the 1990s can be expected to press for better long-term care in the 2000s. "As this generation gets older, we will bring that activism," says Susan Reverby, a self-described baby boomer who is Luella LaMer Professor of Women's Studies at Wellesley College. Reverby predicts increasing concern about such issues as the quality of life in nursing homes. Issues that currently are of great concern among advocates for older people, such as the use of restraints in nursing-home care, can be expected to become larger on the public agenda with the aging of baby boomers.

Many diseases common among women are almost certain to become more prevalent. Cancer is expected to become the number-one cause of death within the decade, and this transition should enhance concerns about breast cancer among women. One measure of such concerns is the $16.5 million that Avon has raised for breast cancer education and awareness programs since the start of its Breast Cancer Awareness Crusade in 1993. A growing number of women with arthritis, diabetes, and heart disease should also make the business of providing good women's health care more urgent.

Prevention will be of greater interest as older women recognize the clear link between exercise, a healthy diet, and the prevention of heart disease. Physicians will be expected to provide more preventive services, both by patients and by insurers. This will require a change in approach, says Dr. Antonia Novello, former surgeon general of the U.S. "For some reason, we have been taught to cure, not to prevent," Novello said at a 1996 conference on women's health.

Screening measures are of growing importance, and physicians can expect increasing pressure from insurers to screen patients for conditions that can lead to serious and costly problems if not treated early. One insurer, Kaiser Permanente of Northern California, has become a national leader in gathering data to show the effectiveness of early screening for colon cancer. Such efforts make sense, says Paul Engstrom of Fox Chase Cancer Center in Philadelphia. "HMOs want to be on the side of preventive medicine. It's also good marketing to show you're putting discretionary dollars into preventive health and screening," he told *The Wall Street Journal*.

Whatever their future work or family arrangements, women will continue to depend on doctors, midwives, hospitals, health clinics, and the manufacturers of products ranging from birth-control pills to tampons. There are still enormous opportunities to offer better medical products and services to women. A huge market awaits the manufacturers of highly effective birth control that protects against sexually transmitted diseases, for example. Women still need menopause therapy for targeted symptoms. And effective arthritis drugs with no gastrointestinal side effects will find a huge market.

Women's complaints about health care remain a serious obstacle for many organizations. Women continue to say they are not being listened to, are waiting too long for appointments, and are being "talked down to" by physicians. These complaints suggest that health providers must change their own staff attitudes to serve women better.

Health marketers are in a squeeze. They face a complicated market with changing needs at a time when the high cost of health care is under fire. Marketing cannot always solve these problems. As managed care increases its hold, larger numbers of women can be expected to switch physicians in order to retain their health insurance. Even providers with loyal patients will see many of their patients change doctors to maintain coverage.

However, effective marketing should help physicians retain patients and make their practices more desirable to managed care providers who also need to market their services to business. Solid relationships with patients, earned by providing good care and offering women what they want, should create a buffer against the harsh environment of contemporary health care.

Health marketing will always be vulnerable to critics who say it is unnecessary. Healers are using money that critics say should be spent on worthier efforts, such as research to cure cancer or efforts to immunize more children. In a 1996 issue of *Harper's* magazine, Greg Critser accuses "pharmo-capitalists" of transforming health care into a system that "each day is devoted less to the art of medicine and more to the delivery of pills."

The essay is a reminder of the perils of marketing health products to men or women. Health marketing that is perceived as "excessive" runs the risk of awakening the public's sense that marketing a public service, such as health care, is unnecessary.

Effective health marketers must come to terms constantly with the shifting, critical sensibility of modern women. At the same time, they must work in an increasingly competitive industry where health marketing is more important than ever. Marketers who use sensitive appeals to women while offering top-quality products and services should maintain an edge over the competition. Good marketing gives hospitals, physicians, and products greater opportunities to help in a crisis, ease suffering, and enhance the lives of women and their families.

Notes on Sources

Several primary sources were used throughout the book. Most predictions of demand for products or services stem from the Census Bureau's *Population Projections of the United States, by Age, Sex, Race, and Hispanic Origin: 1995-2050*, by Jennifer Cheeseman Day. (1996, document number P25-1130). In every case, the middle series of population predictions was used. The actual numbers of babies, menopausal women, and women with arthritis in future years will vary depending on everything from the availability and use of birth control to immigration policy.

The book depends heavily on marketing reports from Find/SVP, a company that also produces all *Packaged Facts* reports. The company's reports on everything from contraceptives to pregnancy tests are thorough and trustworthy. The company is located at 625 Avenue of the Americas, New York, NY 10011.

A number of women's health marketers were primary resources for the book, either through interviews with them, through their written work, through their suggestions for interviews, or a combination of all three.

Ruthie H. Dearing has helped shape women's health marketing for years through her work as a consultant and through her newsletter, *Marketing Women's Healthcare*. Her 1987 book, *Marketing Women's Health Care* (Aspen Publishers, Inc.), looks primarily at hospital marketing. Dearing co-authored the book with Helen A. Gordon, Dorolyn M. Sohner, and Lynne C. Weidel. She is located at Dearing and Associates Incorporated, South 1414 Bernard, Spokane, WA 99203.

Sally J. Rynne helped found many of the first women's health centers at hospitals, and has had a great influence on the field through her

Women's Healthcare Consultants practice, at 500 Davis Street, Suite 700, Evanston, IL 60201; and her health newsletters.

Richard C. Ireland, president of The Snowmass Institute for Strategic Studies and publisher of *The Ireland Report on Women's Health Marketing*, offers an influential forum for women's heath marketers with his wife, editor Peggie A. Ireland. They publish a periodical and hold an annual conference on the subject. They are located at 8694 East Mineral Circle, Englewood, CO 80112.

Other key sources were Mary Anne Graf of Health Care Innovations, 4 Triad Center, Suite 210, Salt Lake City, UT 84180; and Kathleen L. Lewton, a public relations expert at Porter/Novelli, 303 E. Wacker, Suite 1214, Chicago, IL 60601.

Another important source was About Women Inc., whose *Marketing to Women* newsletter and book, *About Women and Health* (1992), offer a broad and valuable cross-section of the world of women's health marketing. The company is located at 33 Broad Street, Boston, MA 02109.

Two studies cited throughout this book are the "The Commonwealth Fund Survey of Women's Health" (July 1993), a survey of 2,500 women and 1,000 men; and the National Survey on Women's Health Decision Making, a survey of 800 women conducted for the Center for Women Policy Studies in September 1994.

Finally, data from Simmons Market Research Bureau and ACNielsen are used throughout the book. Both are highly respected, professional sources of marketing data. Simmons is located at 420 Lexington Avenue, New York, NY 10170. Nielsen's address is 150 North Martingale Road, Schaumburg, IL 60173.

Chapter 1. Focus on Women

Making decisions

2. Women make health-care decisions in 64 percent of American households, according to the 1996 National Research Corporation Healthcare Market Guide. The study draws from 170,000 households in

48 states. The National Research Corporation is located at Gold's Galleria, 1033 O Street, Lincoln, NE 68508.

2. Women make 80 percent of America's chain drugstore purchases, according to the *Chain Drug Review* survey of consumer shopping, from *Chain Drug Review*, July 3, 1995, p.100.

2. The National Center for Health Statistics tracks physician visits. Women made 60 percent of physician visits as reported in the National Center for Health Statistics' Advance Data, No. 253, August 18, 1994.

2. Mary Anne Graf reports from focus groups that women are more likely to choose health insurance than men.

History of advertising

8. Dr. West's advertisement and "The Little Woman G.P.A." from Roland Marchand's *Advertising the American Dream* (Berkeley: University of California Press, 1985), an entertaining and literate exploration of advertising history. West's ad from the *Saturday Evening Post*, October 13, 1934, p. 38, p. 303 in Marchand. Little woman ad from the *Saturday Evening Post*, March 24, 1928, p. 53, p. 169 in Marchand.

Women changing health

9. Eunice K.M. Ernst described the dawning of the women's health movement in "Health Care Reform as an Ongoing Process" in the *Journal of Obstetric Gynecologic Neonatal Nursing*, February 1994, pp. 129-138, Vol. 23, No. 2.

9. *Our Bodies, Ourselves*, first published in 1973, was published in a revised version in 1984 as *The New Our Bodies, Ourselves* by Simon and Schuster, Inc. The same collective that wrote these books, The Boston

Women's Health Collective, also has published *Ourselves and Our Children* and *Ourselves, Growing Older*. All four books are rich with information about health and about what women schooled in the women's health movement want in health care.

9. From *Seizing Our Bodies*, edited by Claudia Dreifus (New York: Vintage Books, 1977).

11. A good overview of the DES tragedy can be found in *DES: The Bitter Pill*, by Robert Meyers (New York: Seaview/Putnam, 1983).

Drug advertising

19. Direct-to-consumer advertising of prescription products data from Leonard Sloane, "Prescription Drug Campaigns Aimed Directly At Consumers Expanded Rapidly During the Last Year," *The New York Times*, January 9, 1995, p. D-7.

Chapter 2. The Future of Childbirth

Childbirth

37. Births by age from National Center for Health Statistics, annual reports of Final Natality Statistics, and Advance Report of Final Natality Statistics, 1994.

39-40. Information about women, midwives, and referrals to midwives was obtained from "How Women of Child-Bearing Age View Certified Nurse Midwives," a 1993 survey of 500 women conducted for the American College of Nurse-Midwives; and "Certified Nurse Midwives Gain Converts," *Marketing to Women,* from About Women Inc., November 1995, pp. 9-10.

39. Changing percentage of babies delivered by midwives from *Women's Health: The Market for Menopause, Fertility, Contraceptive and Cancer Drugs*, Find/SVP, New York, NY, November 1995, pp. 94-95.

42. Prenatal care of Hispanic, black, and other mothers from National Center for Health Statistics, *Vital Statistics of the United States* (annual), *Monthly Vital Statistics* report, and unpublished data.

Infertility

43-45. Information about success rates, cost, and profit status of various infertility centers from Trip Gabriel, "High-Tech Pregnancies Test Hope's Limit," *The New York Times*, January 7, 1996, Section 1, pp. 18-19, the first of a four-part series on infertility. Information also drawn from "Fact Sheet on In Vitro Fertilization" and "Fact Sheet on Infertility," from the American Society for Reproductive Medicine, March 1996.

43-49. The infertility market and insurance coverage is explored in Lisa Gubernick and Dana Wechsler Linden's article, "Tarnished Miracle," *Forbes*, November 6, 1995, pp. 98-101.

44-45. *Data from Women's Health: The Market for Menopause, Fertility, Contraceptive and Cancer Drugs* from Find/SVP (1995); and from Paula Mergenhagen DeWitt, "In Pursuit of Pregnancy," *American Demographics*, May 1993, pp. 48-54.

Chapter 3: A Fertile Market

Marketing to mothers

50. Data about spending during baby's first year of life from Lifestyle Change Communications, 1700 Water Place, Suite 150, Atlanta, GA 30339.

Menstrual products

51. Early Kotex ad from *Ladies' Home Journal*, March 1931, p. 145, cited in Marchand, *Advertising the American Dream*, p. 22.

52. This account of Procter & Gamble's response to the Rely disaster is drawn from Alecia Swasy's insightful and lively book, *Soap Opera/The Inside Story of Procter&Gamble* (New York: Times Books, 1993).

54. Projected sales figures for feminine hygiene products is from *The Feminine Hygiene Market, Packaged Facts,* January 1994.

Contraceptives

61. Lysol advertisement from *Women's Home Companion*, February 1927, p. 182, cited in Marchand, *Advertising the American Dream*, p. 345. Lysol advertisement examined by Marchand, p. 346

62. The fascinating story of the way oral contraceptives changed society is the focus of *The Pill*, by Bernard Asbell (New York: Random House, 1995).

62. Luce quote from "The Dangers of Oral Contraception," by Barbara Seaman, in Dreifus, *Seizing Our Bodies*, p. 79.

62-63. Market figures are drawn from *Women's Health: The Market for Menopause, Fertility, Contraceptive and Cancer Drugs*, Find/SVP, November 1995.

63-64. Contraceptive use data drawn from "Contraceptive Use in the United States: 1982-1990, from *Advance Data, National Center for Health Statistics*, No. 260, February 14, 1995; "Contraception: Trends in Use, Safety and Effectiveness," a fact sheet from "Emerging Issues in

Reproductive Health," a briefing session for journalists, January 31, 1996. The briefing was sponsored by The Alan Guttmacher Institute of New York; The Henry J. Kaiser Family Foundation of Menlo Park, California; and the National Press Foundation of Washington, D.C. Data were also obtained from "A Guide to the Methods of Contraception," an undated document distributed by Planned Parenthood of America, Inc. in 1995.

64-65. Ancient Egyptian condom use is examined by Joseph G. Schenker and Vicki Rabenou in "Family Planning: cultural and religious perspectives" in *Human Reproduction*, Vol. 8, No. 6, 1993, pp. 969-976.

66. Criticism of female condom from Marion Asnes, "Birth Control Over 30," *Working Woman*, July 1994, p. 70.

67. Women's conversations with physicians about birth control from "The Kaiser Family Foundation National Survey on Public Perceptions About Contraception," a survey of 512 women and 488 men released in January 1996.

68. Complaints about contraceptives from JoAnn Rosenfeld, Pamela M. Zahorik, Wendy Saint, and George Murphy, "Women's Satisfaction With Birth Control," *Journal of Family Practice*, February 1993, p. 169.

70-71. Attorney's complaints about Norplant from Geoffrey Crowley, "The Norplant Backlash," *Newsweek*, November 27, 1995.

70-71. Information about Norplant controversy from Jacqueline Darroch Forrest and Lisa Kaeser, "Questions of Balance: Issues Emerging from the Introduction of the Hormonal Implant," *Family Planning Perspectives*, Vol. 25, No. 3, May-June 1993.

Pregnancy testing and ovulation detectors

75-76. Predicted market and sales data from *The Home Medical Test Products Market, Vol. I, Packaged Facts,* March 1995.

76. Quidel Corporation's pregnancy testing strategies examined in Rita Koselka, "Hope and Fear as Marketing Tools," *Forbes,* August 29, 1994, pp. 78-79. Quote from Chief Executive Steven Frankel also obtained from the story.

Chapter 4: Marketing Family Products to Women

79. Health-insurance earnings data from *Source Book of Health Insurance Data 1994,* Health Insurance Association of America, p. 21.

79. Grey Advertising study discussed in Sally Goll Beatty, "Women's Views of Their Lives Aren't Reflected by Advertisers," *The Wall Street Journal,* December 19, 1995.

80. Women's age at childbirth from National Center for Health Statistics, *Advance Report of Final Natality Statistics,* 1994.

81. Increase in single mothers, from "Single Parents," *American Demographics,* December 1993, pp. 36-37.

82. More adult children at home, from "Married with Grown Children," *American Demographics,* December 1993, pp. 32-33; and Susan Mitchell, *The Official Guide to the Generations,* (Ithaca: New Strategist Publications, Inc., 1995), p. 71.

82. Women as primary caregivers examined in Patricia Braus, "When Mom Needs Help," *American Demographics,* March 1994, pp. 38-46.

87-88. Nyquil observations from *Positioning: The Battle for Your Mind*, by Al Ries and Jack Trout (New York: McGraw Hill, 1986), a dynamic look at the psychology of marketing.

92-93. Older people as computer owners, from Mitchell, *The Official Guide to the Generations*, p. 391.

93. Older people as media users from Robert Maxwell, "Videophiles and Other Americans," *American Demographics*, July 1992, pp. 48-55; and Mitchell, *The Official Guide to the Generations*, p. 389.

Chapter 5: Higher Stakes, Hotter Debates

95-97. Menopause market data from *Women's Health: The Market for Menopause, Fertility, Contraceptive, and Cancer Drugs,* by Find/SVP, 1995.

100-102. Information about early menopause knowledge is from Germaine Greer, author of *The Change: Women, Aging and Menopause* (New York: Ballantine, 1993). *The Change* also looks at societal stereotypes about older women, and the author's own unconventional approach to the process.

102. "The Gateway to a Second Adulthood" is from Gail Sheehy, "The Silent Passage: Menopause," *Vanity Fair*, October 1991, p. 252. Sheehy's book of the same title (New York: Random House, 1992) drew public attention to menopause as an important women's health issue.

102. Carol Landau Ph.D., Dr. Michelle G. Cyr, and Dr. Anne W. Moulton are the authors of *The Complete Book of Menopause* (New York: Perigee, 1995), a clear overview of current medical approaches to menopause.

102. Eagerness for information about menopause from Wendy W. Livingston, Joseph M. Healy Jr., Harmon S. Jordan, Cheryl K. Warner, James L. Zazzali, "Assessing the Needs of Women and Clinicians for the Management of Menopause in an HMO," *Journal of General Internal Medicine*, Vol. 9, July 1994, pp. 385-389.

103. Women talking to doctors about menopause, data from Gallup poll of 833 women cited in "Women Need More and Better Information on Menopause from Their Physicians," by Teri Randall, *Journal of the American Medical Association*, October 13, 1993, Vol. 270, No. 14, p. 1664.

105. Premarin sales figures from IMS America of Plymouth Meeting, Pennsylvania, cited in "Delicate Balance: Estrogen Study Shifts Ground for Women," by Elyse Tanouye, *The Wall Street Journal*, June 15, 1995, p. A-1.

105. The percentage of women taking hormone replacement therapy is from 1987, the final year of the Massachusetts Women's Health Study. The study, which covered the years 1981 to 1987, included women who were aged 45 to 55 in the first year of the study. Data from Elina Hemminki, Donald J. Brambilla, Sonja M. McKinlay, and Jennifer G. Posner, "Use of Estrogens among Middle-Aged Massachusetts Women," *Pharmacoepidemiology*, April 1991, Vol. 25, pp. 418-423.

105. Women's risk of death from heart disease compared to death from breast cancer from U.S. National Center for Health Statistics, *Vital Statistics of the United States* (annual), and unpublished data.

107. Marketing of Fosamax examined by Elyse Tanouye in "Merck's Osteoporosis Warnings Pave the Way for Its New Drug," *The Wall Street Journal*, June 28, 1995, p. B-1.

Chapter 6: Older Women, Greater Needs

Two of the sources for this chapter are quoted extensively. Both focus their efforts on marketing to older Americans. They are Frank Conaway, president of Primelife, 127 S. Olive Street, Orange, CA 92666; and Margaret Wylde, president, ProMatura Group Institute for Technology Development, 428 North Lamar Boulevard, Oxford, MS, 39655.

115. Incontinence sales figures from Raju Narisetti, "Marketing: Products to Aid the Incontinent Are Growing Up," *The Wall Street Journal*, November 13, 1995, p. B-1.

117. Data on health spending among older Americans from 1994 Consumer Expenditure Survey, Bureau of Labor Statistics.

117. Hospital use data from "A Profile of Older Americans 1995," American Association for Retired Persons.

119-120. Physiological differences between older and younger consumers from Charles D. Schewe, "How to Communicate with Older Adults," *American Demographics*, August 1991, p. 53; and Patricia Braus, "Vision in an Aging America," *American Demographics*, June 1995, pp. 34-38.

120. Finances of older women from "A Profile of Older Americans 1995" from the AARP; "The Biggest Spenders," *American Demographics*, December 1995, pp. 28-29; 1994 Consumer Expenditure Survey, The Bureau of Labor Statistics; and the Census Bureau's March 1996 Current Population Survey.

123. Richard A. Lee's look at attitudes within the advertising industry toward older people is published in a report, *Ageism in Advertising*, pub-

lished by Lee, High-Yield Marketing, 585 Heinel Drive, Roseville, MN, 55113.

125. Women in the work force data from the Bureau of Labor Statistics, *Household Data Annual Averages 1995.*

126. Women in nursing homes, from the Census Bureau.

126. Older women feeling good, Russell, *The Official Guide to the American Marketplace*, p. 33.

127. Hospital closing data, from *Source Book of Health Insurance Data*, p. 119.

127. Hospital discharge data. From U.S. National Center for Health Statistics, *Health, United States, 1994*, and unpublished data.

Arthritis and Painkillers

131. Future arthritis prevalence. *Morbidity and Mortality Weekly Review*, May 5, 1995 and June 24, 1994, The Arthritis Foundation; unpublished data from the Centers For Disease Control and Prevention and Census Bureau projections.

132. Launching new painkillers, from "Marketing: Nonprofit group's name to go on for-profit pills," by Pamela Sebastion, *Ad Age*, July 13, 1994.

133. New pain relievers on the market, from Joseph Weber and Zachary Schiller, "Painkillers are about to O.D.," *Business Week*, April 11, 1994.

133. Bufferin sales drop from "Turmoil over Painkillers, but Smooth Seas for Investors," by Milt Freudenheim, *The New York Times*, March 24, 1996.

134. Number of new drugs in trials, from "New Medicines in Development for Women 1994," the Pharmaceutical Research and Manufacturers of America.

134. Alternative therapy use from David M. Eisenberg, Ronald C. Kessler, Cindy Foster, Frances E. Norlock, David R. Calkins, Thomas L. Delbanco, "Unconventional Medicine in the United States," *The New England Journal of Medicine*, January 28, 1993, Vol. 28, No. 4., pp. 246-252.

Incontinence

136. Incontinence data from "Managing Acute and Chronic Urinary Incontinence," No. 2, 1996. The Public Health Service, Agency for Health Care Policy and Research.

137. Sales of incontinence products from the *Progressive Grocer* "1995 Non-Foods Sales Manual," August 1995, pp. 106-108.

Long-Term Care

139-141. Homecare information from "Basic Statistics About Home Care 1995," National Association for Home Care, Washington, D.C.

143-144. Marketing of long-term care from the *Marion Merrell Dow Managed Care Long Term Digest* 1993.

145-146. Long-term care in the future is explored in "Taking Turns at the Crystal Ball," *Nursing Homes*, February 1996, pp. 11-19.

Chapter 7: Women's Health Centers

The major source of information about the history and current operation of women's centers is a study from Jacobs Institute of Women's Health by Carol S. Weisman, Barbara Curbow, and Amal J. Khoury, "The National Survey of Women's Health Centers: Current Models of Women-Centered Care" in *Women's Health Issues*, Vol. 5, No. 3, Fall 1995. The study offers a wealth of information and a broad look at the subject.

157. HMO and family-planning-center relationship data from "Reproductive Health Services and Managed Care Plans: Improving the Fit," The Alan Guttmacher Institute, March 1996.

Chapter 8: From Exercise to Echinacea

162. Sales figures of organic foods and natural products from the "14th Annual Market Overview," *Natural Foods Merchandiser*, June 1995, pp. 1, 62-64.

163. The prevalence of stories in magazines looking at nutrition and other preventive health strategies was explored in "Magazine Watch," in *The Ireland Report on Women's Health Marketing*, November-December 1995.

164. Women's exercise and eating habits have been documented annually in *The Prevention Index* since 1983. Sixty-six percent of women polled for the 1996 report said they do not exercise strenuously for at least 20 minutes three days a week or more. National Survey on Women's Health Decision Making conducted for the Center for Women's Policy Studies.

164. Link between added weight and heart attack in women from Jane E. Brody, "A Bathroom Scale Shows Coronary Risk," *The New York Times*, February 8, 1995.

167. Walking and gardening rates from John P. Robinson and Geoffrey Godbey, "Has Fitness Peaked?" *American Demographics*, September 1993, pp. 36-42.

169. Estimates of echinacea sales from Geoffrey Crowley, "The Natural Drug Culture," *Newsweek*, May 6, 1996, pp. 61-68.

174. Percentage of Americans who are sedentary, from Jane E. Brody, "More of the Elderly Seek the Benefits of Exercise," *The New York Times*, October 4, 1995.

Chapter 9: Moving Ahead

177. Database marketing from Jonathan Berry with John Verity, Kathleen Kerwin, Gail DeGeorge, "Database Marketing, A Potent New Tool for Selling," *Business Week*, September 5, 1994.

178. Privacy data from the *Equifax-Harris Mid-Decade Consumer Privacy Survey*, 1995, based on 1,006 telephone interviews conducted by Louis Harris and Associates, Inc.

179. The "Microbe Killer" and other early advertising from Paul Starr, *The Social Transformation of American Medicine* (New York: Basic Books, Inc., 1982).

179. Profit and marketing observations from Donald Drake and Marian Uhlman's critical analysis of the pharmaceutical industry, *Making Medicine, Making Money* (Kansas City: Andrews and McMeel, 1993).

179-180. Merck sales and philanthropic record from Merck 1995 Annual Report.

182. Data examining sources of health information from "Health Care—For Advice: Family Doctor Or 'Dr. Mom.'" *Roper Reports*, September 1995, pp. 22-23 and 340-354.

183. Denver's After-Hours Care Program, discussed by Bruce E. Johnson, Barton D. Schmitt, and John H. Wasson, "Taming the Telephone," from *Patient Care*, June 15, 1995, pp. 136-156.

186. "HMOs want to be on the side..." from Marilyn Chase, "Health Journal: California HMO Pushes Screening for Colon Cancers," *The Wall Street Journal*, March 25, 1996, p. B-1.

187. Greg Critser's essay about the marketing of medicine, "Oh, How Happy We Will Be," from *Harper's*, June 1996, pp. 39-48.

Index

About the Author

Ms. Braus is a regular contributor to *American Demographics* magazine, and her articles have appeared in *Parenting, Rochester Business Magazine, Ms.,* and *The New Physician.* She has also contributed to the *Gale Encyclopedia of Science* and reported on health care and science for daily newspapers. Ms. Braus holds degrees from Cornell University and the University of Rochester. She lives in Rochester, New York with her husband and two sons.

AMERICAN DEMOGRAPHICS BOOKS

Marketing Know-How: Your Guide to the Best Marketing Tools and Sources

This comprehensive, information-packed guide tells you everything you need to know about your customers and how to reach them, plus an expert's prospective on forces that will drive consumer markets into the next century. Hundreds of sources are organized by their primary function: federal, state, and local government; international; nonprofit; academic; business-to-business; data vendors; software providers; publishing; market research services; GIS suppliers and more.

Targeting Transitions: Marketing to Consumers During Life Changes

Millions of Americans go through major life transitions each year, including getting married or remarried, becoming parents and grandparents, changing careers, getting divorced, moving, becoming caregivers, and retiring. Once you understand the characteristics of people in transition, you can begin to discover the marketing opportunities created by these events.

Everybody Eats: Supermarket Consumers in the 1990s

This is the first book to focus exclusively on supermarket shoppers and factors that influence their food purchasing decisions. It divides shoppers into four age segments: mature consumers, baby boomers, baby busters, and hidden influencers (young children and teenagers). It further divides consumers in terms of region, race and ethnicity, and economic groups. Learn how different groups of consumers respond to new products and how you can help consumers manage the sea of product information they face every time they enter the supermarket.

The Baby Bust: A Generation Comes of Age

As a generation, busters are unique in their experiences, beliefs, politics, and preferences. This is the first statistical biography of this generation. It tells the baby bust's story through demographics, opinion polls, expert analysis, anecdotes, and the indispensable comments and experiences of busters themselves.

Segmenting the Mature Market

People over age 50 account for 43 percent of all U.S. households and half of all quantitative discretionary income. Learn how and where seniors spend their money, what cars they drive and where they go, who is retiring, and who is returning to work. Find out about their media preferences, health-care concerns, and enormous political influence.

Targeting Families: Marketing To and Through the New Family

Word-of-mouth product recommendations made from one family member to another are significantly more effective than those made between friends or colleagues. Learn how to get family members on your sales force and how to implement a "Full Family Marketing" approach that attracts youths, spouses, and seniors.

Beyond Mind Games: The Marketing Power of Psychographics

The first book that details what psychographics is, where it came from, and how you can use it.

Selling the Story: The Layman's Guide to Collecting and Communicating Demographic Information

A handbook offering a crash course in demography and solid instruction in writing about numbers. Learn how to use numbers carefully, how to avoid misusing them, and how to bring cold numbers to life by relating them to real people.

The Seasons of Business: The Marketer's Guide to Consumer Behavior

Learn which demographic groups are the principal players and which consumer concerns are most pressing in each marketing season.